The Poems of St. George Tucker
of Williamsburg, Virginia—1752-1827

St. Memin engraving of St. George Tucker done in 1807. Tucker-Coleman Collection, Earl Gregg Swem Library, The College of William and Mary in Virginia.

The Poems
of
St. George Tucker
of Williamsburg, Virginia
1752-1827

Collected and Edited
by

William S. Prince

VANTAGE PRESS
New York   Washington   Atlanta   Hollywood

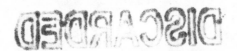

FIRST EDITION

Copyright © 1977 by William S. Prince

Published by Vantage Press, Inc.
516 West 34th Street, New York, New York 10001

Manufactured in the United States of America
Standard Book Number 533-02618-0

167528

Dedication

To the Memory of Norman Holmes Pearson

Contents

Preface

History has remembered St. George Tucker of Williamsburg, Virginia, as a distinguished jurist, but has forgotten him as a poet. And yet, to his contemporaries, he was as well known and respected as a poet as he was a judge. His good friend and fellow versifier, Governor John Page of Virginia, once assured him that "your poems . . . will give you more credit with posterity than the invention of a telegraph."

But posterity has forgotten both the telegraph Tucker invented and the more than two hundred poems he wrote during his lifetime. The telegraph is forever doomed to oblivion, and posterity is no worse off for that. The poems, however, are deserving of a better fate, and it is with that conviction that a selection of them has been revived and offered to the public.

The first of Tucker's poems dates from 1773, when he was twenty-one, the last from 1823, when he was seventy-one. By "first" and "last," I mean those poems that have survived in manuscript. My guess is that these are the first and last poems because Tucker seems to have had the efficient jurist's habit of keeping everything he wrote, and of affixing the precise date of composition as well. Thus, his two hundred poems are the fruit of fifty years of verse writing, from the last days of Great Britain's rule in the colony of Virginia, through the administrations of Washington, John Adams, Jefferson, Madison, Monroe, and ending in the second year of the administration of John Quincy Adams.

The poems, then, come out of the "times that try men's souls" and out of that less dramatic, but no less trying, time after the Revolution—a time that might be labeled one that "tried men's minds"—when the war over the emerging nation's political philosophy was bitterly fought by Federalists and Jeffersonians. Tucker, a young officer in the local militia during the closing years of the Revolution, had sharpened his pen in the service of his country with a couple of anti-British satires, and then plunged headlong into the political battle during the bitter struggle between Jefferson and Hamilton with his "Jonathan Pindar" poems in 1793. The specialist in American political history will find these fourteen "odes" of great interest, but so, I hope, will the ordinary reader, for Tucker did not write them for the specialist—he wrote them for "Mr. Citizen," for the American of his day, and although some of the references in them are lost on us, we cannot fail to feel the passion and appreciate the humor in these, the best of Tucker's compositions. "The Probationary Odes of Jonathan Pindar, Esq." were published for the first and last time in 1796, so their emergence in this volume salvages them from 180 years of neglect.

Also included in this volume is a selection of Tucker's personal lyrics, societal verses, patriotic "hymns," and ribald ballads and tales. These last are unique. There is nothing like them in American literature for this period. Readers acquainted with the genteel poetry from eighteenth-century New England will find Tucker's bawdy rhymes a startling addition to our country's literary heritage!

In selecting the poems for this collection, I have asked myself two questions: which are Tucker's best poems? and, which poems are the most interesting? By "best" I mean having the most literary worth. By "interesting," I mean having the most historical worth—to the reader interested in the literary, social, or political history of the United States.

But some will ask, "Do *any* of Tucker's poems have literary worth?" And my reply is another question, "Do *any American* poems of this period have literary worth?" Certainly Tucker was no Whitman, say, but neither was John Trumbull or Joel Barlow or Timothy Dwight or David Humphreys. These, the "Connecticut Wits," along with Philip Freneau, all contemporaries of Tucker, are the poets whose works posterity has chosen to preserve. Do their poems have literary worth? Trumbull is remembered for his satire "McFingall," and Barlow for "The Hasty Pudding," but no one will argue that either is "great" poetry.

Of course, in poetry, as in all art, what is "good" to one is trash to another. T. S. Eliot loathed Poe—who is admired by many who dislike Eliot. Except for that rarified being, the Critic, whose judgment is made on a plane far above that of most mortals, personal taste, personal feeling is all. So I have selected those poems of Tucker's that seem to me to have the power to appeal to the heart and mind of the reader today. And I think that many of them do have that power. Insofar as they do, the poems are "good."

Those poems that are not "good" are "interesting" for one very good reason—they are from the pen of a Southerner. Here is a large body of poetry, from the South of the late eighteenth and early nineteenth centuries. That fact alone makes them worth reviving, because there is so very little literature from the South of this period. One college anthology of American literature, published in 1970, offers selections from Trumbull, Dwight, Barlow, and Freneau, Northerners all, but nothing from any contemporary Southerner. Another more prestigious one, now in its third edition, offers only Freneau's verses. The *Oxford Anthology of American Literature* prints no poems at all from the South of this period.

As I have said, Tucker had the habit of keeping everything he wrote. His descendants, in their turn, preserved his manuscripts, some in his house, which may still be seen on Nicholson Street in Williamsburg, some in their own homes in other cities. Now, most of Tucker's manuscripts and many of his letters are gathered together in the Tucker-Coleman Collection in the Earl Gregg Swem Library of the College of William and Mary in Virginia. There, in a handsome room given by the Coleman family, are many of the books from Tucker's own library. An oil painting of Tucker, copied from a contemporary engraving (frontispiece), hangs over a glass cabinet containing a few memorabilia—Tucker's watch, the water jug he carried on his judicial rounds, a watercolor of the doorway of his birthplace in Bermuda.

About a hundred—half—of Tucker's extant poems are preserved just as he jotted them down, some on mere scraps of paper. A few are to be found in his letters. The rest are in four manuscript volumes. These contain all the poems that he considered his best work. They are carefully written out in his own hand. Three of the volumes are handsomely bound in green leather and tooled in gold.

As Tucker kept almost everything he wrote, so he dated almost all of his poems. These dates are given under the poems, on the left. Dates of first publication, if any, are given on the right. If Tucker did not date a poem, and I have been able to do so, the date is given in brackets.

xi

With the exception of the punctuation, the text of the poems has been modernized. This has consisted, chiefly, in changing the spelling to conform with present American usage, spelling out contracted words and abbreviations, and reducing to lower case the initial letters of nouns that do not require capitalization. In some cases, Tucker's spelling has been retained where a change would impair the rhyme or meter of the line.

I would like to thank Mr. William C. Pollard, librarian of the Earl Gregg Swem Library of the College of William and Mary in Virginia, for granting me permission to copy Tucker's manuscripts, to quote from the Tucker-Coleman collection, and to reproduce the St. Memin engraving of Tucker. I should also like to thank Miss Margaret Cook, manuscript librarian at the Earl Gregg Swem Library, for her assistance, and Mrs. Edith McFarlan and Mrs. Marjorie Blair for typing the manuscript. I am indebted to the administration and faculty of Pacific University for granting me the sabbatical leave that gave me the time to finish the project.

INTRODUCTION

St. George Tucker was born in Bermuda in June, 1752, the youngest son of Colonel Harry Tucker, retired, of His Majesty's Forces, and the member of a family whose name went back to the beginning of Bermuda's colonial history. When St. George was twenty years old, he followed his two older brothers to America. The eldest, Thomas Tudor, having received his law degree in Edinburgh, had taken up residence in Charleston and was joined there in 1771 by brother Nathaniel[1] who, known as the poet of the family, hoped to compose the epics that would bring him both fame and fortune. He was to die in Scotland thirty-seven years later, an impoverished physician, better known for his translations of Swedenborg than for *The Bermudian* (1774) and a half dozen other poems.

St. George enrolled in the College of William and Mary at Williamsburg, then the capital of colonial Virginia, and in 1773 began the study of law under the famous statesman and jurist, George Wythe. He was admitted to the practice of law before the General Court the following year, and on May Day, 1775, had his license signed by the royal governor, Lord Dunmore. It was one of Dunmore's last official acts before the turbulent events of the summer of 1775 forced him and his family to leave forever the palace and Virginia.

Before the young lawyer had the opportunity to hang out his shingle, the same forces that had removed the royal governor from his palace also precipitated St. George into a life of adventure and action such as he was never again to experience. While some Virginians were forced to make agonizing decisions as to which way they would go—stay with the "rebels" or leave with Dunmore—St. George was one of those young men who apparently never had a doubt about whose side he was on. For the first two or three years of the war, he aided the American cause by operating four small ships, transporting indigo to Bermuda and the West Indies in exchange for arms and ammunition. In 1778, he married Frances Bland Randolph, the young and very eligible widow of John Randolph of Matoax, and gave up his career as a blockade runner, but continued to serve the cause by enlisting in the local militia. He participated in several battles, including the siege of Yorktown and witnessed the capitulation of the British forces.

Tucker was twenty-nine years old when the war ended. In those nine years he had established for himself a secure place in Williamsburg society. He had earned a degree from the socially prestigious college; he had become a member of the bar; he had served his new country in the war; he had made money and he had married an eminently eligible widow. But these acts alone do not explain his success. Two years after he came to Williamsburg, the president of the Council in Virginia had written to St. George's father congratulating him on "having a son whose good sense, cheerfulness of disposition, and goodness of heart have recommended him in a strange country to the notice of the most respected persons among us."[2] The young man's verse-writing ability must have pleased his new friends, too. He soon became known as a clever rhymster who could pay charming tribute to a young lady about to be married, as he did in "Written on Miss Cocke's Wedding day" (p. 37), in 1775, or who could wittily satirize the Tory enemy, as in "The Alarm" (p. 76), in 1776. The first few lines of "A Dream on Bridecake" (p. 42) indicate that by 1777 Tucker's reputation as a poet was prompting his friends to turn to him when verses were desired: "Dear girls, since you the task impose / Of scribbling rhyme. . . ." This reputation grew with him, leading out from this doggerel written for a wedding party to serious elegies on the deaths of friends or public figures, patriotic poems to be sung on public occasions, and political satires to be printed in the public press. Typical of these later requests that Tucker had is one contained in a letter from William Wirt, former attorney-general of the United States, in 1814—thirty-seven years after the "girl's" request to scribble rhyme. Referring to the "infamous meeting" of the Federalists in Hartford, Wirt pleaded, "Can't you write something?"

Tucker's marriage to Frances Bland Randolph was undoubtedly beneficial socially, since both the Randolphs and the Blands were leading families in Virginia. But the match was also a love affair that lasted for the ten years of their life together. Tucker first saw Frances on November 13, 1777, and resolved then and there he would marry her. In the following ten months he composed several poems to her, addressing her as "Stella," in imitation of the English poet Shenstone's *A Pastoral Ballad* (1743). He married her on September 23, 1778. From that day until her death in 1788, Tucker wrote Frances poetry, often composing a verse-letter to her as he jostled along in his coach on his judicial rounds. The grief he felt when she died on January 18, 1788, is expressed in two poems, one of which he wrote at her grave.

In her ten years as Tucker's wife, Frances bore him three sons and three daughters. Two daughters died in infancy; the third, Frances Tucker Coalter, died at the age of thirty-four in 1813. One of the three sons died at twelve; the other two survived to become famous jurists in their own right. Both of them emulated their father by serving in high offices before the bar, and in holding professorships at the College of William and Mary. Henry St. George (1780-1848) also served a term each in both the state senate and the U.S. House of Representatives. His brother, Nathaniel Beverly (1784-1851), was a prolific writer on law and political economy. He also wrote poetry and published three novels, one of which, *George Balcombe* (1836), received high praise from Edgar Allan Poe.

In 1791, Tucker married another socially prominent widow, Lelia Carter, the daughter of Sir Peyton Skipwith. The three children by this union all died in childhood. The marriage was a happy one but seems to have lacked the romance of the first. There are no poems addressed to Lelia.

For a half-dozen years after Yorktown, Tucker practiced law in the general courts. In 1788, the year of Frances's death, he was elected one of the four judges of the General Court, but he resigned from that post two years later when he was invited to succeed his former teacher, Wythe, as professor of law at the College of William and Mary. Tucker held this post for thirteen years, and distinguished himself as a teacher and a scholar. One of his students wrote that "he is more luminous on the subject of law than any man I ever saw," and that he can with "ease and familiarity clear up or eliminate any knotty point of law, and he not only possesses the capability of doing it, but does it with willingness."[3] Another student paid tribute to his teacher's eloquence and enthusiasm in a cartoon which survives among Tucker's papers. It depicts a rather gaunt man, seated at a desk. His right arm is raised, forefinger up, mouth open, hair disheveled. On the desk are his pen, a sheef of notes, and two books (p. 4).

The books might be two of the five-volume edition of *Blackstone's Commentaries* that Tucker published in 1803. This scholarly work was a standard text in Virginia for many years.[4] In it Tucker discusses the application of English common law, as interpreted by the famous English jurist, Blackstone, to the laws of Vir-

Student cartoon of St. George Tucker, done beween 1790 and 1800 when he was Professor of Law at The College of William and Mary. Tucker-Coleman Collection, Earl Gregg Swem Library, The College of William and Mary in Virginia.

ginia and the United States. Additionally, Tucker includes several essays of his own, setting forth his views on the "Several Forms of Government," and the "Right of Conscience, and Freedom of Speech, and of the Press." During his tenure as professor of law, he also wrote and published, both separately and in the contemporary press, essays on slavery,[5] trade,[6] and the Louisiana Purchase.[7] All of these writings reveal his strong republican principles, his patriotism, and his humanitarianism.

In 1804, Tucker resigned from the faculty of the College when he was elected to the High Court of Appeals to fill the vacancy created by the death of Edmund Pendleton. This position required him to spend more of his time in Richmond than in Williamsburg, so when, in 1811, his duties were extended to keep him away from home for even longer periods of time, he resigned. A poem he wrote in 1810 humorously expresses the discontent that led to his resignation the following year. It is entitled "The Sorry Judge" and is set to the tune of "The Jolly Miller." Here is the first stanza:

There was a sorry judge who lived at the Swan by himself,
He got but little honor, and he got but little pelf,
He drudged and judged from morn to night, no ass drudged more
    than he,
And the more he drudged, and the more he judged, the sorrier judge
    was he.

So he returned to his beloved Williamsburg, and for two years enjoyed the company of his wife, children, and friends, but once again donned judicial robes when he accepted, in 1813, the appointment as judge of the United States Court for Virginia. He held this office until shortly before his death in 1827. He died in November, one year after John Adams and Thomas Jefferson.

Like his more famous contemporary, Thomas Jefferson, Tucker was an eighteenth-century man of many accomplishments. Besides being a judge, teacher, essayist, and poet, he was also an enthusiastic amateur astronomer and inventor. His notebooks contain elaborate calculations and diagrams of the movements of the planets and of ideas for machines like the semaphore that he offered to Governor Cabell of Virginia.

At his death, Tucker left a personal library of about 500 volumes. Less than a quarter of them were law books. The rest were

5

histories or narratives of exploration (about 100); philosophy—Hume, Rousseau, Montesquieu, Locke, Voltaire; several multi-volume sets of English and American periodicals; and literature—Latin, English, French, and American. Tucker owned copies of Richard Savage's *The Wanderer,* James Thompson's *The Seasons,* the poems of Peter Pindar (John Wolcot), Burns, Goldsmith, Akenside, Dryden, Butler, Milton, and Chaucer. And although their works were not in the inventory of his library, his poems prove that he was familiar with the poetry of Pope, Shenstone, Young, Collins, Gray, Prior, and Shakespeare. All of these English poets flourished in the eighteenth century or earlier. The great Romantic poets—Keats, Shelley, and Byron—were all Tucker's contemporaries, and all died before he did, yet there is no evidence that he was acquainted with their poetry. Neither does he seem to have read Cowper, Blake, Coleridge, or Wordsworth. Of American poets, Tucker owned volumes of Trumbull, Robert Munford, and Philip Freneau, and his writings show that he knew the works of Barlow, Hopkins, and Humphreys, but there is no indication that he had ever read any of Bryant, whose first volume of poetry came out six years before Tucker's death.

In other words, the English poets that Tucker knew best, and who shaped his style, were the neo-classic poets of the eighteenth century, the "Augustans," while the American poets familiar to him were the "Connecticut Wits," whose verse also followed eighteenth-century conventions. Briefly, those conventions consist, in subject matter, of a concern for the general over the particular, for man rather than individual men, for society rather than nature. In style, this poetry is marked by personifications of abstract qualities ("Happiness," "Tyranny"), poetic diction ("deign," "thee," "ere," "whilst"), classical allusions, and regularity of meter and rhyme.

Modern poetry is intensely personal. The reader looks over the poet's shoulder. But the poetry of Tucker's age was social. Poetry was thought of as an art, not as private confession. The problem, then, for the poet was clearly to distinguish his poetry from prose, and he did this by employing the conventions listed above. Since the poet steered away from immediate and direct contact with experience—the personal—he sought to induce emotion in his readers by means of a sort of social code. When Tucker personifies "Happiness," or "Tyranny," he is asking the reader to share with others the emotions engendered by the general, universal aspects of these states. So, too, the classical allusions allowed all of his educated (a social norm!) readers to ground their reactions on a common base of reference.

Tucker's poems also remind us that his was an oratorical age. Speeches of that time were marked by high-flown rhetoric, classical allusions, and Latinisms. A much-published poet of the day, Mrs. Mercy Warren, wrote speeches for some members of Congress. When William Wirt recited one of Tucker's patriotic odes from the steps of the state capitol in Richmond in 1807, he could do so because the style of the poem was in harmony with the political oratory of that place.

Like the ode that Wirt recited, the thirty or so other poems that Tucker submitted for public consumption are all of a social nature. They are political satires, or patriotic odes, or lyrics and elegies on people or events in the public eye. The only "personal" poems that he had published were a half-dozen that were included with those of Margaret Lowther's (later, Mrs. John Page) in her *Journal,* privately printed about 1790, and "Resignation," his best-known poem which was printed without his knowledge. And none of the published poems, social or personal, bore his name. The nearest he came to admitting to the authorship of a published poem was to allow a *"T"* to appear at the end of it. When he sent a copy of his elegy on the burning of the Richmond theater to the Richmond *Enquirer,* he asked the editor neither to show it to anyone nor to tell anyone who the author was.

Tucker strongly believed in the social worth of poetry, and of literature in general, but he feared that "a taste for the belles-lettres . . . is very low in America generally." So he wrote to William Wirt in 1812 when Wirt, then engaged in writing a play, asked Tucker how he thought his professional standing might be affected if it became known that he was the author of a play. Tucker went on to say that literature didn't "constitute anything estimable in the public eye, nor advance the author in the public estimation, *but may have the contrary effect"* (Tucker's emphasis). He said that if the author were a professional man who had already won the public's respect, he might get away with tossing out a poem as "the effusion of a leisure moment . . . or an offering at the shrine of party." Then it would "advance him in the general estimation as a man of happy genius."

Tucker was not a great poet. He was an imitator, not an experimenter. That he did not write better poetry is partly to be explained by his own lack of native genius, and partly by the coercions of the times. As he said to Wirt, writing poetry didn't "constitute anything estimable in the public eye. . . ." He was not encouraged to experiment by a public that measured all poetic effort against the standard of English neo-classic verse. And yet, he had the artistic impulse. He worked hard to perfect his art. Many of his poems, especially the longer ones, exist in multiple drafts. Words are crossed out, others substituted, whole stanzas are changed as many as four times, and experiments are made with combining one poem with another.

The sympathetic reader—and all poetry needs such a reader—will find pleasure in these poems. Not as much, of course, as Tucker's contemporaries did, for there is a gap of two centuries separating us from his readers. It is a gap filled with changes in thought and feeling that sets us apart from Tucker's contemporaries, and fills us with demands we make upon literature that the literature of their day did not have to confront. Indeed, the psychological and social complexities of our age are too great for anything but great poetry. Tucker's readers lived in a simpler, more optimistic age. Taking for granted more "Truths" than we, they looked for confirmation of those truths in their art, and their art pleased them insofar as they found them there. To us, these Truths emerge as clichés. But is that Tucker's fault—or ours?

Poems Among Friends

In and around Williamsburg in the last half of the eighteenth century lived the "bourgeois aristocracy" of the Chesapeake society. At a time when there was no "South" in the sense that we know it today, this Chesapeake society was one of several modes of existence in the southern area of colonial America. It existed as a more or less distinct geographical unit, and differed from the others around it economically, politically, and socially. Here lived the great tobacco planters with their mansions, their libraries, their coaches, and their slaves. Here, too, lived the men who ran the machinery of the colonial government and then that of the state and national governments: the Washingtons, the Jeffersons, the Pages, the Randolphs.

For eighty years, until 1775, Williamsburg was the colonial capital, the permanent or temporary residence of the burgesses and assemblymen and their families, and, of course, of the royal governor. The presence of these governmental officials, and of the faculty and students of the College, created a gay social life that attracted others to the town for prolonged visits. For five years, until 1780, the town was the capital of the Commonwealth of Virginia. It was moved to Richmond in that year because Williamsburg was considered to be too vulnerable to a British attack from the sea. Although the removal of the capital caused the population to dwindle from about 2000 to 1200 in sixteen years, the society of Williamsburg maintained its former gentility. An English visitor to the town in 1795 wrote that "the society in it is thought to be more extensive and genteel at the same time than what is to be met with in any other place in America."[8]

In this society, where large families were the rule (Tucker sired nine children), large gatherings of families and friends were normal. Young and old amused themselves with dancing, singing, and amateur theatrics. One of Tucker's own plays was performed on the evening of March 21, 1815, before an audience consisting of "the whole Tucker fireside, and was received with great applause." A poem not in Tucker's hand, but among his manuscripts, describes a musical evening in the Tucker house. It begins with what is probably a portrait of Tucker: "A tall slanky fellow / Played the violin-cello," and goes on to name the other amateur musicians: Coalter (Tucker's son-in-law), who played the Welch harp; Miss Blair, who played the fiddle; "my dear Abby," who played the harpsichord; Jenny, who played the flute; and one of the Nelsons, who played the timbrels.

Because of the great distances friends had to travel, and the lack of public accommodations, weddings were more often performed in the home of the bride than in church. Consequently, guests often came early and stayed late. Singing, dancing, and feasting were the diversions on these happy occasions. "The Cynic" (p. 138) probably gives a typical menu for one of these wedding feasts. The number and variety of delicacies listed suggest that the Virginia gentleman and lady enjoyed the pleasures of the table. Wedding breakfasts were occasions for the reading of verses inspired by sleeping on the wedding cake. Two of the "Dreams" are in this collection (pp. 42 and 43).

Picnicking, too, provided Tucker and his friends rest and diversion from their duties. A poem written as a letter to William Nelson, in 1795, describes a "sweet entertainment" he had the misfortune to

9

miss. The company drove out of Williamsburg in three "chariots," spread a carpet in an orchard, set up a table, and laid out the feast—bread and iced butter, apoquimini cakes, "a delicate shad," cold ham, broiled chicken, sherbet, and negus. After this breakfast, the picnickers lay about and conversed until the July heat sent them back to town with much hilarity (p. 58).

Another of Tucker's verse-letters (p. 58) amusingly describes the excitement generated in the ladies by the arrival of a "cargoe of ribbons and gauzes and shoes." Although organized amusements were infrequent in post-colonial Williamsburg, the ladies could look forward to decking themselves out for balls at the College and even dances on the Palace Green (p. 70). The town seemed to have more than its share of pretty girls. Tucker paid tribute to nine of them in "The Belles of Williamsburg" (p. 38), a poem that made a big hit at the time. And of course in this college town there were handsome young men, too, for the "belles" to flirt with, as they did—even in church (see "Lines," p. 70).

Flirting in church might have been thought of as a breach of manners in this society, but not as a sin, as it surely would have been in New England. In 1787, the Yankee preacher, Jedediah Morse, visited Williamsburg in search of information for his American *Universal Geography*. When he recorded in that work that there was "very little appearance of religion in Williamsburg," Tucker was outraged. In *A Letter to the Rev. Jedediah Morse, A.M.*, published as a pamphlet in 1795, he sarcastically asked, "Did he expect to see a procession like the triumphal entry of St. Rosolia at Palermo . . . or the celebration of an Auto de Fe at Madrid. Or did he expect to hear the ministers of Christ calling out loud like the prophets of Baal, cutting themselves with knives . . . and leaping upon the altars." He went on to say that he was happy that his congregation could listen silently to their minister, pray with "inward fervor," and avoid "extravagant manifestations of zeal."

Tucker's God is benevolent and generous, one who both rewards and forgives. Religion is synonymous with morality. It is by man's social conduct that God will judge him. In "Written on Christmas Day, 1820" (p. 75), Tucker says that Christ was born

> To teach frail man to serve,
>   and love his God, above,
> Nor from that path to swerve.
>   His neighbor next to love.

He goes on to say that it is man's duty to relieve the wretched, exalt the humble, comfort those who grieve, forgive faults, clothe the poor, and feed the needy. Finally, man must put his trust in God and "leave to him the rest." Implicit in the poem is an acceptance of a natural order of social stratification. God accepts this order, but he puts certain obligations on those at the top—on the gentlemen.

A part of this "natural order" was the institution of slavery, and the Tucker household had its quota of slaves. Like all sensitive men of his time, Tucker was concerned about the slavery "question." In 1796 he published an essay, *A Dissertation on Slavery,* in which his premise was that if slaves were freed, and deprived of all civil rights, they would gradually emigrate to the unsettled Southwest where they would set up their own, all-black society. When the United States acquired the Louisiana Territory, Tucker suggested that slaves be settled there. He wrote only one poem on the subject of slavery, however. This is "A Fable" (p. 68). It suggests the uneasiness he must have felt about his "natural order."

This was a stable society, then, with ordered ways and few challenges to his equilibrium. It was a society that enjoyed good food and drink, music and dancing, art and literature. It was a society that enjoyed the pleasures of the senses but one that was not sensual. Tucker's notes to his poem "To Tyranny" (not in this collection) show strong disapproval of the loose and cynical morality of the English nobility. At the same time, Tucker shared with other members of his society, both men and women, an earthy sense of humor. The existence of the ribald tales proves this, as does the fact that he thought nothing of reading "A Second Dream on Bridecake" (p. 43) to a mixed company.

Among Tucker's papers are poems that were written by more than two dozen of his friends. Three with whom he was most active in verse-writing were John Page, Page's wife Margaret, and William Wirt. Both men held positions of great public responsibility. Wirt was attorney-general under Monroe and John Quincy Adams, and Page was a U.S. congressman and the governor of Virginia for three terms. Though like Tucker, busy with the demands of their offices, both men found the time for literary composition. Remembered for his "Old Bachelor" essays, Wirt also wrote a comedy called "The Path of Pleasure," and exchanged rhymed epigrams with Tucker on topical subjects. Tucker's verse-writing with Page began before 1790 and continued to Page's death in 1808. In 1790, the same year as her marriage to Page, Margaret Lowther published a *Journal* of a trip she

11

had made up the New England coast a year or two before. In it are eighty-five poems: forty-one by John Page, twenty-eight by Margaret, and sixteen by Tucker. When her husband died, Mrs. Page moved away from "Rosewell," the Page estate on the York River, and settled near the Tuckers in Williamsburg. There she and Tucker continued to participate in their mutual hobby. One year a dreary sequence of rainy days inspired an exchange of sixteen poems.

Some of the poems that Tucker composed for his friends on special occasions have already been mentioned, such as the one for Patsy Cocke's wedding and the "Dreams" on the wedding cake. He wrote poetry for less happy occasions, too, such as when the Wirts' son died in France in 1825. Composed for a larger audience, for the Chesapeake society as a whole, are five elegies that Tucker wrote between 1779 and 1812. One was inspired by a public calamity—the burning of the theater in Richmond—the other four by the deaths of prominent citizens. At least two of these poems received contemporary publication, one in Virginia and the other in New York. But with their stilted, artificial diction, these are the least successful of Tucker's compositions. None is printed in this collection.

More pleasing are some of the personal lyrics that Tucker wrote. There are about forty of these. About half are light songs or odes; the remainder are serious verses inspired by Tucker's meditations on "Life," and by the emotions he experienced as a father and husband.

Tucker's poem "The Sorry Judge" has already been mentioned. This was set to the familiar tune of the old song, "The Jolly Miller," and is one of several poems that Tucker adapted to familiar tunes. This practice of writing new verses for old tunes was a vogue of the late eighteenth century. Robert Burns, whose poems were first published in 1786, was the best and the most famous "song" writer of the day. Tucker was directly influenced by Burns's lyrics. He wrote a poem called "An Imitation of Robert Burns," another in Scottish dialect, and a third, "To Genius," a tribute to the Scotsman. These he sent to George Thomson, in Edinburgh, the editor of *A Select Collection of Original Scottish Airs,* hoping to have them printed. But Thomson replied with a polite rejection slip.

"Be Merry and Wise" (p. 73), "Bacchanalian" (p. 71), and "Anacreontic" (p. 73), "written while shaving in the morning," are all cheerful, spontaneous lyrics. "Burletta" (p. 64), is possibly, Tucker's most original poem. It successfully evokes that feeling of being kept in a state of semiconsciousness by the annoying buzzing of flies around one's pillow.

12

Most of Tucker's serious personal verses are marred for us by an excess of rhetoric and sentiment. Perhaps the most spontaneous of them in this collection is "To Sleep" (p. 48), written just six days after the death of his first wife, Frances. Using Thomas Gray's stanza (immortalized in "Elegy in a Country Churchyard"), and the direct, simple diction of Gray, Tucker achieves a pleasing blending of form and feeling. The sincere tone of quiet grief established in the first stanza is maintained to the end of the poem. "Hymn to the Creator" (p. 50), written in 1790 and published two years later in *The American Museum,* is one of four or five religious poems. It is as near to a personal expression of religious feeling as Tucker ever attempted. But there is no preaching. There is only the expression of his wonder at the mysteries of creation, and his inability to fathom the mighty scheme of things.

"Resignation" (p. 63) is probably Tucker's best-remembered poem. It appealed to the sensibilities of Tucker's generation, both in this country and in England. It was frequently included in anthologies of poetry in the latter half of the nineteenth century. A measure of its popularity may be gained from the fact that a copy was found among the papers of Dolly Madison,[9] the president's wife, at her death, and from the extravagant praise it received from ex-President John Adams. Writing to a friend who had sent him the poem,[10] Adams said that "I know not which to admire most, its Simplicity, its Beauty, its Pathos, its Philosophy, its Morality, its Religion, or its Sublimity." He then asked, "Is there in Homer, in Virgil, in Milton, in Shakespeare, or in Pope, an equal number of lines which deserve to be engraven on the memory of youth and age in more indelible characters?" And he concluded by confessing that he would rather be the author of the poem than of Joel Barlow's "Columbiad."

Adams asked the friend, Richard Rush, for information about Tucker. Rush conveyed Adam's praise and the request to Tucker, who sent Rush—rather surprisingly—none of his own poetry, but two poems by his brother Nathaniel and his own pamphlet on slavery. Neither did he tell Adams that he was the author of the anti-Federalist satires, *The Probationary Odes of Jonathan Pindar* (p. 82), in which he had referred to Adams, who was then vice-president, as "daddy-vice," "would-be great man," and "most superfluous highness." Party factionalism was behind them both. The Muse that would have been the cause of dividing them, had they ever met, was now the means of uniting them in a bond of friendship. Such is the power of Poetry!

The Satires

The use to which the eighteenth-century English gentleman put satire was well understood by Tucker. Since the days of Butler, Dryden, Swift, and Pope, satire had been the weapon of the gentleman poet. Nor was the tradition lacking in vitality in Tucker's own time. Churchill's *The Candidate,* attacking Lord Sandwich, had appeared in 1764. In the 1780s there had been printed in the English press "The Criticisms of the Roliad" and "The Probationary Odes" of Richard Fitzpatrick, Lord John Townshend, George Ellis, R. Tickell, and others. These had been followed by the verses of John Wolcot attacking Pitt and George III. Satire had crossed the Atlantic, too, and found hospitality in the colonies. The newspapers of the day were full of satiric verse. Among Tucker's papers is a newspaper clipping dated 1788 of Francis Hopkinson's mock-epic satire, "The Battle of the Kegs" (1778). Tucker knew, too, the satirical poems of the Connecticut Wits: "McFingal" (1776) by Trumbull, and *The Anarchiad* (1786-1787) by Trumbull, Barlow, Hopkins, and Humphreys.

Tucker's satirical verses fall into three main groups: those aimed at the British, those aimed at the Federalists, and those aimed at particular persons or institutions irrespective of their national or party connections.

The first of Tucker's poems written to ridicule the British was "The Alarm," composed in Bermuda, in June, 1776. Tucker had sailed for Bermuda in June of the preceding year, and remained there until November of 1776. During this time hostilities broke out between the colonies and Great Britain. "The Alarm" (p. 76) is a humorous account of the consternation caused among the loyalist guests at a banquet given by the governor, when a report reached them that Esek Hopkins, commander-in-chief of the fleet of the United States, had landed on the island. The report was not true, but the rumor was enough to send the dignified company scurrying off "as mice desert their cheese. . . ."

"The Alarm" is one of a half-dozen satires inspired by wartime incidents. The best of them is the parody (p. 78) of Lord Cornwallis's proclamation that Tucker wrote "in camp, March 20, 1781," five days after the battle of Guilford Court House, in which Tucker fought.

The British lost twice as many men as the Americans at this battle, but because the militia was routed, Cornwallis considered it a

British victory. Accordingly, on March 18, he issued *A Proclamation,* offering to accept back into the fold any rebels who, "having seen the errors into which they have been deluded by falsehoods and misrepresentation, are sincerely desirous of returning to their allegiance. . . ." Tucker took this proclamation and produced a versified imitation of it which cleverly distorts the sense and tone of Cornwallis's message, and makes him appear in a ridiculous light.

Tucker's parody of Cornwallis's proclamation is unique. There are contemporary parodies of Burgoyne's proclamation of July 4, 1777, one attributed to Hopkinson, but only Tucker's for Cornwallis's.

Tucker's verses on Merino sheep entitled "A New Song" (p. 116) are not dated, but there is evidence that they were written in 1810. The poem satirizes the current rage for this brand of sheep, originally brought into the United States in 1801 by David Humphreys. Letters which Jefferson wrote in 1809 show that he was eager that the stock of Merino sheep in this country be increased.[11] He believed that by improving the quality of wool produced, the United States could be emancipated from its dependence upon foreign manufacture. Therefore, when, the next year, the sheep began to fetch exorbitantly high prices (up to a thousand dollars each), Jefferson was indignant, and wrote to Madison wondering if there were not some way to halt the speculations.

Some idea of the interest there was in Merino sheep can be gained from an ad that was printed in the Richmond *Enquirer* on September 21, 1810, and repeated eight times in October, nine in November, and five in December:

Merino Sheep . . . —Just imported, in the schooner *Greyhound,* Capt. Baxter, from Lisbon, ONE HUNDRED AND FOURTEEN
MERINO SHEEP,
which were shipped by Wm. Jarvis, Esq. U.S. Consul—They are to be landed tomorrow, and pastured at Fairfield, where they may be seen—For terms of sale, and other particulars, apply to
Samuel Myers.

Just as these advertisements must have dinned the words "Merino sheep" into Tucker's consciousness, so, in "A New Song," he dins them into the reader's. In the twelve stanzas of this poem he repeats "Merino sheep" forty-five times, "sheep" nine times, makes every verse-ending rhyme with "sheep," and employs similar internal rhymes.

Tucker had a penchant for writing satirical verse, but he did not attempt to reach a wide audience until he began to write his odes in imitation of Peter Pindar, in 1793. Before 1793, he appears to have been content to let off steam against persons and events simply by writing the verses, perhaps showing them to a few friends, and then putting them aside. But to the man whose correspondence frequently bore the salutation "Citizen St. George Tucker," the events of the first years of Washington's administration called for more than gentlemanly dabbling. John Page was writing to a sympathetic audience when, on June 3, 1793, he wrote to Tucker to thank him for an epigrammatic ode:

> 'Tis devlish good. I itch to give it to Freneau. He has been beforehand with you in an attack both in prose and verse—I do not recollect the signatures of the pieces, but I told my wife that if it were possible for you to have sent them to the press I would say you had written them. Indeed the cause of republicanism or of humanity stands in need of every exertion of its friends—But for the glorious efforts of our French allies, I should almost dread the extirpation of Liberty. Our general govt. as it is called was running headlong into monarchy. I hope the new Congress will check this madness.

Page's suspicions were justified. On June 1 there had appeared in Freneau's *National Gazette* the first of Tucker's fourteen satirical odes printed in that paper during the summer of 1793. "Citizen St. George Tucker," masked as "Jonathan Pindar," had gone into the lists to fight for republicanism.

Like the newspaper for which some of them were originally written, *The Probationary Odes of Jonathan Pindar* are violently anti-administration in character. In order properly to understand them, it is necessary to know something of the events of the day which provided Tucker with his subject matter.

In 1793, the Washington administration was beginning its second term. Under the leadership of Alexander Hamilton, secretary of the Treasury, Congress, striving to establish a strong, centralized government, had passed bills which were intended to put the federal government on a firm financial footing. These had provided for the funding of the national debt, the assumption of the state debts, and the establishment of a national bank.

Hamilton had outlined his plans for the funding of the national debt in his "Report of the Public Credit," read to the House and Senate in January, 1790. Under the terms of this bill, government certificates, which had been issued during the war, were to be redeemed at par, payment to be made from the proceeds of a tax levied on the people as a whole. Naturally, this bill had the backing of those wealthy members of society who foresightedly had purchased large amounts of certificates. And during the period when the bill was being debated, speculation in certificates was rampant. Certain members of Congress and their friends seized the opportunity to purchase script from its original holders. Since most of these holders, being ignorant of the government's intentions, considered their paper worthless, they gladly sold it to the speculators for as little as three shillings on the pound.

There were many, like Tucker, who firmly believed that these congressmen, backed by the moneyed interests, had forced the bill through purely for their own benefit. Lacking the perspective which time gives to events, they saw only that the speculators had made a killing, while the original holders of certificates, the ex-soldier, the farmer, and the small merchant, were worse off than before. Not only had they lost their securities, but they were to be taxed to pay the interest on the script now in the hands of these speculators.

The South was bitter about the funding scheme for several reasons. For one, most of the speculating gentry were Northerners. For another, the states with the largest unpaid debts were in the North: Massachusetts, the center of Northern political power, had the greatest debt of all, while Virginia had paid off most of her debt. Why, asked Tucker—and every Southern property-holder—why should Virginia be taxed to help pay the debts of Massachusetts? That seemed grossly unfair. Furthermore, he disliked the idea of the federal government's becoming the states' creditor, for he feared that state governments would then be in perpetual obligation to "Washington."

As it was opposed to Assumption, so the South was opposed to the establishment of a national bank, for it feared that the bank would lead to the concentration of money in the North, the center of commerce—and Federalism. When the Bank Bill was passed and

17

signed into law (1790) and the directors named, Southerners like Tucker were more than ever convinced that the government had only the interest of a select few at heart, for the directorships seemed to go to all those congressmen who had favored the establishment of the bank, to men like Fisher Ames, Rufus King, and William Smith.

The opponents of Hamilton had other reasons as well for opposing the bank. Madison challenged the constitutionality of such an institution, pointing out that the constitution did not authorize to Congress the power to establish banks. Hamilton replied by invoking the doctrine of implied powers. In doing so, he further alarmed those who felt that the government already wielded power in too arbitrary a manner. If Hamilton could imply the power to establish a bank, what powers could he not imply? To these critics, the establishment of the bank was another ominous indication that the government was assuming monarchial tendencies.

In 1793, there were many who shared John Page's alarm, expressed in the letter he wrote to Tucker, that the government was "running headlong into monarchy." Not only had the policies of the administration caused Page and others to feel as they did, but there were other indications of monarchial tendencies. John Fenno's *The Gazette of the United States,* the acknowledged organ of Hamilton, favored titles of distinction for the heads of government. It was well-known that John Adams, the vice-president, had thought the title of "President" unsuitable to the dignity of that station. Then, too, there had been Adams's "Discourses on Davila," printed in Fenno's journal, which seemed to favor a monarchial over a republican government. The ostentatious conduct of some congressmen, first at New York, then in Philadelphia, and the inclination of high society to treat them as if they were members of the nobility, further convinced some people that the country had but thrown off the cloak of a foreign monarchy to wear one of its own tailoring.

Nor were these critics so sure that the heads of their government did not favor throwing in their lot with "mother Britain." Everyone knew that John Adams was an Anglophile, and he was, after all, the vice-president. Hamilton, the secretary of the Treasury, had given a cool reception to Genet when the latter, in June, 1973, had come to Philadelphia to solicit the United States' backing of the French Republic. And that same month, writing in Fenno's paper under the name of "Pacificus," Hamilton had urged and justified a policy of neutrality toward France. To men like Tucker, who compared

France's struggle to that of the American colonies, Hamilton's "neutrality" was a one-sided affair favoring England in particular and the cause of monarchial government in general.

The fourteen odes by Tucker which were printed in the *National Gazette* in 1793 reflected these attitudes. Both the theory and the practice of the administration are hit. Congress as a body is attacked; individuals are censured. In these odes are crystallized the opinions of all those who opposed Hamilton's measures. From the man in the street, who knew no more than that he was being taxed to pay for the redemption of script in the hands of the rich, to the Virginia planter who viewed askance the efforts of the federal government to make its power supreme. Tucker's verses spoke to every discontented citizen.

As a Virginia and a states-rightist, Tucker criticizes the efforts of Congress and the judiciary to make the states subservient to the federal government. He challenges Congress's right to establish a bank and asserts that the bank exists only for the pecuniary benefit of a few men. He hits out at secret debate, Congress's right to give titles, new loans for foreign nations, standing armies, and taxes. He accuses Congress of speculation, and singles out Hamilton, William Smith of South Carolina, Secretary of War Knox, and Fisher Ames as the chief offenders.

The arch-villain in the piece is, of course, Alexander Hamilton. Nicknaming him "Atlas," Tucker ironically describes his omnipotence. Jay, the Chief Justice, is called "Minos," the mighty judge whose judiciary is swallowing up the states and making waste paper of the Constitution. Vice-President Adams, the "would-be great man," is satirized for his love of titles and self-love. He is chief among the "well-born," the aristocrats, whom Tucker attacks for their anti-republican, pro-English sentiments.

Tucker's odes attracted both delighted partisans and violent critics. On June 29, 1793, after seven had appeared, Jefferson wrote to Madison that "The Probationary Odes (written by S.G.T. in Virga.) are saddled on poor Freneau, who is bloodily attacked about them."[12]

With the appearance of a "Supplementary Ode" in the *Gazette* on September 7, Jonathan Pindar said good-bye to his public. Tucker had intended to submit another series to the *National Gazette,* but the paper ceased publication in October. Most of the odes in the second part of the collection were written during the winter of 1793-1794. By far the most amusing of these is Ode XI, "A Trip to St. James's"

(p. 107). The others are, for the most part, variations of the themes treated in the first series.

The Probationary Odes of Jonathan Pindar are written in imitation of the verses of Peter Pindar, Wolcot's pseudonymn. In using the name Jonathan, the contemporary equivalent of Uncle Sam, Tucker implies that he is the American equivalent of Peter. Peter Pindar satirized the English king and the person and policies of his minister, Pitt. Tucker satirizes Hamilton, the American "king," his policies and his sycophants: Adams, Jay, Fisher Ames, and the rest.

It seems obvious that Tucker chose Peter Pindar as his particular model because his verses were well-known in America. The number of Wolcot's poems which crop up in the newspapers of the time, and the following announcement, printed in *The New York Magazine,* in 1790, suggest that his poems were popular:

> In compliance with the wish of several of our respectable patrons, we shall insert in our department the poetical works of the celebrated Peter Pindar.

The satires, Parts I and II, were published in Philadelphia, in 1796, by Benjamin Franklin Bache. Bache, the editor of *The Aurora,* was a Republican. His paper was the chief organ of the Jeffersonians after Freneau's *National Gazette* shut down its presses in 1793. Since none of the manuscripts of Tucker's odes is annotated, it was probably Bache who contributed most of the "notes, critical and explanatory, by Christopher Clearsight, Esq." Bache also may have had a part in editing the poems. When Page was arranging for their publication, he wrote to Tucker that *"B"* had them but could not publish some parts and wanted to strike out at least ten lines. Page added that he would leave it to the discretion of Bache and Mr. Giles to make the corrections.

It is appropriate that Giles should have had a part in the publication of Tucker's poems, for he was one of Alexander Hamilton's chief opponents. The representative from Virginia, Giles had opposed the Bank Bill in 1791, and in 1793 had been picked by Jefferson to lead the opposition to Hamilton's financial measures. Giles may well have been the author of some of the notes in which the financial policies of the administration are criticized in some detail.

Tucker was so secretive about revealing his authorship of the odes that even Page, before he learned that Bache was the printer, mistakenly took some corrections, which Tucker had sent him, to Matthew Carey. For a great many years the impression prevailed that, because the poems had been printed in Freneau's paper, Freneau was their author. When the odes were appearing in the *National Gazette,* Tucker tried to dispel this impression by adding a notice to "Ode V." It read in part, "Jonathan hereby (in due form) exculpatheth the editor of the *National Gazette* for the horrid and damning charge of writing the Probationary Odes."

As an eighteenth-century gentleman, a responsible citizen, and a man of literary talent, it was natural that Tucker, in the 1790s, should have turned to satire. Tucker was culturally an Englishman, and for a good hundred years satire had been the weapon used by literate Englishmen in the defense of their civil liberties. Furthermore, being educated in the classics, Tucker was aware of the role satire had played in ancient Rome. Copies of Horace and Juvenal were in his library. When Tucker prefaced several of the Odes with quotations from Horace, he was not showing off his learning. Horace was read and respected by every educated man. In quoting his words, Tucker was indicating the good company his own kept. In a sense, he was justifying them by placing them in their genre.

It is his political satire, particularly *The Probationary Odes,* that Tucker is at his best. The *Odes* are party verses, and they vibrate with the passions which Tucker felt. The author of these verses is not the St. George Tucker of the patriotic poems, but closer to the Tucker of the Tales. The political satires are characterized by the same robustness that is to be found in "The Tobacco Pipe" and "Humps and Robin."

The Probationary Odes make what would appear to be the only political satires written by a Southerner during the early national period. In addition, they are the only ones which deal at any length with the important national issues of that period. Yet, they have remained generally unknown to students of American literature and history alike. It is usual to cite *The Anarchiad* as the satirical poem which best describes the unsettled condition of the early years of the Republic. But *The Anarchiad,* written in 1786 and 1787, gives only a preview of the exciting times that were to come.

The Probationary Odes were written by a Virginian, by an anti-Federalist. But they more truly reflect the state of the American mind between 1781 and 1800 than does *The Anarchiad.* The "Wits," perhaps because they were written too soon, perhaps be-

21

cause they were (with the exception of Barlow) Federalists, did not, in their poem, fully grasp the significance of such issues as Shays's Rebellion and the paper-money controversy. They did not see that the real issue was not whether government was going to triumph over anarchy, but that it was what *kind* of government was going to be established. In the thirteen years following the Federal Convention of 1787, the issue which split the country was whether there was to be a strong, centralized government run by the rich and the well-born, or whether there was to be a government of defined and limited powers administered by the elected representatives of the people as a whole.

By 1793 this issue was clearly defined. It had become the all-important and all-pervasive concern of every thinking American. Because it is the theme of *The Probationary Odes of Jonathan Pindar,* this work is unquestionably more deserving of the epithet, "a national poem" than is *The Anarchiad.*

The Patriotic Poems

Tucker's purpose in his patriotic poems is to remind Americans of their glorious past and to alert them to their present responsibilities. Although only twenty-one—about ten percent—of Tucker's extant poems are "patriotic," they are major works of his in that he spent more time and effort in composing them, in rewriting them, and in trying to publish them, than he did on his satires or other poems. In this group, too, are his longest compositions.

In "Liberty" (not in this collection), the longest, Tucker sets forth the major theme of these poems, the mission of America. The 270 lines of this poem were written in 1780, during the Revolution, and dedicated to Washington and "his fellow citizen." The twenty-seven stanzas narrate the progress of the goddess Liberty from her home in Greece to Italy, to Switzerland, to the Netherlands, and to Britain. In each country her stay is brief, for Tyranny and Oppression always force her to move on. Finally, leaving Britain, "The Muse, transported, wings her airy way, / To where Columbia's rising states appear." But even here Britain threatens Liberty, so she rallies the Americans to her defense. After predicting the triumph of Liberty, Tucker warns, "Columbia, then beware the fate of Greece, / Nor let internal broils thy strength destroy!" If Americans heed this warning, "Columbia then shall live to deathless fame / Unrivalled or by Rome or Britain's vaunted name!"

The mission of America is the theme of another of Tucker's long patriotic poems, "Ode for the Fourth of July, 1784" (not in this collection). Beginning with Columbus, Tucker names the explorers who discovered America and began the colonization of her shores. Next he introduces the many fathers of his country: Penn, the Adamses, Henry Witherspoon, Hancock, Franklin. Finally, he lists the famous battles of the Revolution and the "gallant chiefs" and "generous heroes" who "for their country bled."

One of the objects of this poem, as it was for "Liberty," was to warn his countrymen against internal discord. It was a warning he was to sound again and again in his patriotic poems, for union and harmony were not automatically assured with the defeat of the British at Yorktown in 1781. Shays's Rebellion in 1789, the Virginia and Kentucky Resolutions in 1798, and the Hartford Convention in 1814-1815 were all symptoms of the many "internal broils" that threatened Columbia's future. Sometimes his warning takes on a note of urgency, as in "Ode to Union," which was finished two months after the declaration of war against Britain in June, 1812. In this poem, Tucker cautions that "civil war and civil strife" are more to be feared than war with Britain, and he pleads for unity: "Columbia! let thy fierce dissensions cease! / Let union lead thee to the abodes of peace!"

Britain is, of course, the arch-tyrant in nearly all of these patriotic verses, while the hero is Washington. He is the subject of four of the poems, and is glowingly praised in six others. To Tucker, he is "Columbia's hero," "Columbia's proudest boast," "Columbia's chief," "Liberty's favorite son," "the country's ornament" and "shield," and "godlike" Washington who has won "endless life" and "endless glories." And since these are patriotic poems, not party or sectional verses, in only one of them does Tucker speak of Washington as a Virginian. In this, and in their use of classical idiom, these poems are like the majority of "Washingtoniana" written by Tucker's contemporaries.

Like most neo-classical poets, Tucker stresses the general truth, not the particular incident. Thus, the poem on the battle of Princeton contains few allusions to the actual battle. The bulk of the poem gives an allegorical account of the selection and favor of Washington by the Goddess of Liberty. "On General Arnold" (p. 121) reveals none of the circumstances of Arnold's treachery. The drama of his meeting with Major André, André's capture, and Arnold's flight are ignored. To Tucker, these are of no importance. What counts is the meaning of Arnold's act—a sin so horrendous that "Judas [will] be forgot in Arnold's name." Similarly, the lines "For the Fourth of July, 1807" (p. 125), though inspired by the attack of the frigate *Leopard* upon the ship *Chesapeake,* contain no references to the incident. Tucker assumes that his readers know the story. What matters is the *meaning* of the episode: that once again liberty is threatened. In this poem, as in all the others, Tucker is the prophet, not merely the narrator, and is thereby very much like his contempoary bards in New England.

As everyone knows, our national anthem was written to a tavern tune. Several of Tucker's patriotic poems, like his lyrics, were meant to be sung to familiar tunes. Tucker explained in a note to the first of two poems entitled "On General Washington" (p. 120) that it "was written soon after the ascension of George the Third. . . ." William Wirt, U.S. attorney-general from 1817-1829, and Tucker's friend and fellow versifier, has almost certainly identified the original song, for he wrote Tucker asking him to send a "copy of your song in honor of Washington" which he thought went "to the tune of 'The Death of Wolfe'." The first draft of "Invocation" (p. 129) bears the notation that it was to be sung to the "tune—'Scots Wha Hae wi Wallace Bled'." "Union March," written a week before "Invocation," was to be set to the "tune—'Remember the Glories of Bryan the Brave'." The verses entitled "For the Fourth of July, 1804" were "sung at the celebration . . . by a voice noted for its melody."

The culmination of Tucker's many adaptions of verses to songs, and the work that most vividly reveals the fervor of his patriotism, is his musical drama, *The Times, or the Patriot Roused,* which he completed on December 15, 1811. Nine of his patriotic poems are sung in the play. Like the poems, the play is intended to stimulate patriotism and unity of purpose. The five principal characters are Colonel Trueman, his daughter Amanda, his niece Louisa, his best friend Friendly, like him, an "old Revolutionary Officer," and Amanda's "earthly all," Henry. Amanda sings the first song, "Come sweet peace!" and is followed by her father who sings, "No glory I covet, no riches I want." These two songs set forth America's tripartite blessings: peace, personal freedom, and the simple life—blessings that are not found in Europe, as Louisa reminds us in the next song, "O'er the regions of Europe, from Spain to the pole." Colonel Trueman then sings the second of Tucker's two poems on

Washington, and is followed by a "youth" who, with a mixed chorus, sings the song that was originally entitled "Ode for the Fourth of July." Trueman sings the other song on Washington, then a "body of volunteers, dressed in the American light infantry uniform . . . draw up pointing to the audience, and sing"—

> Remember the days, when fair Liberty's call
> Roused the sons of Columbia to arms;
> When we swore, one and all, at her altars to fall,
> Ere a tyrant should rifle her charms.
> When Montgomery, Warren, and Mercer the brave,
> Sealed the thrice solemn oath with their blood;
> And Washington, destined his country to save,
> Swept off all her foes, like a flood.

The play approaches its climax with the dramatic singing of "Invocation." First a chorus of "Washington volunteers" sing the first stanza to Trueman and Friendly: the "Sons of Freedom, who have bled." Then Trueman and Friendly join the Washington volunteers in singing the next song to the young men of the village: the "Sons of patriots in the grave." Finally, a grand chorus consisting of the volunteers, Trueman, Friendly, Amanda, Louisa, sailors, and young men and women all sing the last two stanzas. "The chorus being ended,"

> solemn aerial music is heard behind the scenes. After some short time the curtain rises slowly, and discovers a beautiful transparent scene, in which the figures of Washington, Franklin, Warren, Montgomery, Mercer, Greene, and other distinguished characters of the Revolution appear, as in the skies, surrounded by a glory. The volunteers and villagers of both sexes, Trueman, Friendly, and the rest upon the stage, turn around, and look at the scene in astonishment. The music ceases for a few moments—After a short pause, the following hymn, or march ["Union March"] is sung behind the scene, to a solemn, martial, tune; Trueman and the rest looking all the while as rapt in wonder and admiration.

Here is patriotic drama elevated to the pitch of religious ritual:

25

Washington, Franklin, and the generals of the Revolution become deities, Trueman and Friendly become high priests, and the audience become worshippers.

At the conclusion of the War of 1812, Tucker wrote a sequel to *The Patriot Roused* called *The Patriot Cooled,* but only one of its songs was by Tucker; the rest were "all borrowed from late newspapers." One of the borrowed songs was Francis Hopkinsons's classic Revolutionary satire, "The Battle of the Kegs."

Although Tucker's output of patriotic poems was not large, consisting of only twenty-one poems over some forty years, mere numbers do not reveal the intensity of his struggle with this genre. Several of the poems were reworked as many as four times over twenty-three years. One explanation for this tinkering might be that Tucker was trying to freshen up old manuscripts so that they could be published. A less cynical explanation is that he was using his artistic creations as ammunition in his continual battle to preserve the Union, and that in his rewriting of the poems he was striving for the most effective mode of using them to achieve his purpose. If one accepts this explanation, one might then conclude that Tucker was only a propagandist, and that he harnessed Art to Nationalism. In a sense this was true, but his didacticism did not smother his artistic sensibilities, for the evidence shows that he blotted many a line in his struggle for excellence. The long poem, "Ode for the Fourth of July, 1784," finished in 1812, went through three metamorphoses. "The original design," he wrote, "was for a secular ode for the year 1800, the conclusion, nearly, of the second century since the discovery of the American continent by Europeans." This final draft, only twelve stanzas long, was entitled "Ode for the Fourth of July, 1800." In 1804, Tucker changed and enlarged it, including part of "To Tyranny" and "Ode to Union." He changed the title of the new poem to "Ode for the Fourth of July, 1803," because, he explained, "the Fourth of July, 1803, may be regarded as the period when the United States of America attained the summit of political prosperity; that day, in addition to all former sources of happiness, being announced to them the peaceful acquisition of the immense territory of Louisiana. . . ." So the poem stood, until 1812, when Tucker again worked on it. The sections from "To Tyranny" and "Ode to Union" were discarded, many more names were added to the list of patriots and heroes, and the poem was given its final title.

Other poems were also rewritten several times. "To Tyranny,"

26

first a part of "Ode for the Fourth of July, 1794," was begun in 1798, changed in 1801, revised again in 1812, and put into its final form in 1821. "The Warrior's Song" was written in 1817 but not completed until 1821. The first draft of "Liberty," written during the winter of 1780-1781, is three stanzas shorter than the final version printed in 1788. Even after the poem was published, Tucker was not satisfied with stanza XVII. Among his manuscripts are four different versions, dated June 14, 1794; July 2, 1794 (two); and December 12, 1806. Since Tucker had already published this poem, his reason for reworking this stanza must have been to satisfy his own, purely artistic impulse.

As the years rolled along, and the "sons of patriots in the grave" grew to maturity, Tucker's patriotic poems assumed an increasing importance to him. Determined that the sons should not forget the principles for which their fathers had fought, he began in 1804 to consider publishing a volume of his "poetical pieces, relating to our Revolution," for which he suggested the title, "Occasional Poems, Relating to the Revolutionary War, and Subsequent Events, in the United States of America, since the Establishment of their Independence." Later, sometime after 1817, he drew up a table of contents for a collection of some of his patriotic poems. Beginning with "Liberty," which was to have been the title of the collection, there are twelve poems.

This list may have been compiled as late as 1823. The day after Christmas of that year, Tucker wrote to Matthew Carey, the Philadelphia publisher and author, suggesting that he publish a volume of Tucker's patriotic poems. "Though past the age of seventy-one," Tucker wrote, "I still maintain a warm feeling in the cause of Liberty, and an unextinguishable hatred to tyrants, and their sycophants and agents." He reminded Carey that he had published several of his poems in his *American Museum,* and suggested that these, plus some others, could be collected and published. All proceeds would go to the relief of the Greeks in *their* war of independence, on Tucker's behalf, but not in his name. Tucker enclosed copies of "To Tyranny" and "Ode for the Fourth of July, 1784." But Tucker was not in good health. The task of copying the poems was too much for him. "I know," he wrote, "not a person in this obscure place [Williamsburg] that I could hire to transcribe [the poems] for me." There is no record that Carey ever replied to his letter. It must have been one of the biggest disappointments of Tucker's life that the "quarto edition upon fine paper" was never published.

The patriotic poems of St. George Tucker are products of the Age of Reason. The personifications of abstract qualities, the Latinisms, the classical allusions and quotations, the voluminous notes—all these are used to present Judge Tucker's "case" for his country, just as he used them in his satires to present his "case" for his party. But although the case is presented in the language of the educated reader, it is solidly based on the virtues of the Common Man who lives the Simple Life. An educated man of considerable wealth and high social rank, Tucker yet liked to think of himself, as he once wrote, "an humble poet, born in a remote corner of the earth," a sort of Virginian Horace. Like Horace, Tucker praised the bucolic virtues—or, rather, what he imagined the bucolic virtues to be: simplicity, humility, restraint, hard work. "Be poverty and toil thy envied lot," he sings in "Liberty," for with wealth and ease come "ostentation," "avarice," and "lust," and then the triumph of Tyranny over Freedom. Thus, the patriotic poems are based on a vision of a people who, blessed with political freedom, can only preserve that freedom so long as they continue to live a virtuous life. In short, Tucker bases freedom on individual moral responsibility.

By thus equating morality with freedom, Tucker was establishing a philosophical basis for the logical extension of the Mission of America, a theme that I have said pervades these patriotic poems. In Tucker's poems, the theme has two parts: in the beginning, Freedom found her home in America; next, America kept this freedom by virtuous living. The third part of the theme, not in Tucker but logically following, is that America has a moral obligation to help other *virtuous* but oppressed peoples to obtain their freedom. This part of the Mission was formulated after Tucker's death by statesmen rather than by poets. It has strongly influenced our thinking and our actions up to the present day.

Tales and Anecdotes

In his lively book, published in 1705, *The History and Present State of Virginia,* Robert Beverly relates that while walking in the woods one day he discovered a flower whose form closely resembled the "Pudenda of a man and woman lovingly joined as one." Thinking it "unpardonable to omit a Production so extraordinary," Beverly lured a certain "grave gentleman" out of his way to see "this rarity" and was much amused at the grave gentleman's embarrassment.

Just as Beverley's friend was unprepared for this earthy strain of humor in him, so the reader may be surprised to find the same trait in Tucker. After all, he was "Judge" Tucker and "Professor" Tucker, and judges and professors are assumed to be men whose thoughts never descend from their lofty realm to that vulgar level where the thoughts of ordinary mortals dwell. But Tucker wrote a score of bawdy poems—twenty-three, to be exact—over a period of thirty-four years. Less than one a year, true, but the point is that he was writing them when he was in his sixties just as he was when he was in his thirties. In other words, the kind of humor that characterizes these poems was as much a part of Tucker's personality as it was of Beverley's.

Both men were Virginians, "Cavaliers," if you like, certainly not Puritans. No poems like these are to be found in New England of the time. One could argue that the Connecticut Wits *might* have written some bawdy tales, and not preserved them, but considering the Wits' religious background, and their social milieu, that is hard to imagine. Can one conceive of Joel Barlow, for example, writing a poem like Tucker's "The Cynic" (p. 138)? Not only is the joke too bawdy for the likes of Barlow, but the gourmet's delight with which the Southerner describes the treats laid out for the wedding feasts is totally foreign to the Northerner, who, while living in Paris, the epicure's nirvana, wrote "The Hasty Pudding" (1793), 187 nostalgic couplets in praise of mush!

Ten of the twenty-three humorous pieces that Tucker wrote are, like "The Cynic," little more than anecdotes. But whether they relate only one incident or develop a situation with a series of incidents, these poems stem from a long tradition of the bawdy story. As a literary subject, bawdry has gone out of style. There are no modern counterparts of Bocaccio, Rabelais, Chaucer, or La Fontaine. Matthew Prior, one of the last poets of eminence to work in this genre, died in 1722, a generation before Tucker was born. But the taste for his ribald verses lived on into Tucker's day. Thus, in 1788, Tucker began "Humps and Robin" (p. 130) with these lines:

> O Muse, who didst ere while inspire
> The merry strain of Matthew Prior,
> Descend and to my pen indite
> A tale, which Matt, alone, should write.

For his first sally into this genre, Tucker was probably reacting to the vogue that was stimulated by the publication of Bishop Percy's *Reliques of Ancient English Poetry,* published in 1765. This book made no lasting impression on Tucker as it certainly did on Scott, Coleridge, and Wordsworth, but the fact that there was a copy in his library indicates his acquaintance with the old English ballad. Of more immediate influence on him was a literary ballad published in London in 1785. This was Richard Paul Jodrell's *The Knight and Friars*, a narrative poem dealing with the grotesque incidents involving the corpse of a libertine monk. After reading Jodrell's poem, Tucker wrote a version "in American dress." *The Knights and Friars, an Historical Tale* was published in New York in 1786.

Tucker's poem is in sixty-five ballad stanzas, whereas Jodrell's was in 142 couplets. The most interesting thing about both poems is that they were written by educated men and appealed to educated readers. What seems like crude stuff to us today apparently was then the cause of thigh-slapping laughter in the polite societies of both London and Virginia. That this must have been the case is given weight by the fact that Tucker sent a copy of his tale to Jodrell, who wrote on the back of the title page,

> The Author of the Version was Mr. Saint George Tucker, a Native of America, and Resident in Virginia. He sent me this poem in a parcel from Mr. Wythe of Williamsburg; and it arrived in London on March the 21st 1787.[13]

"Mr. Wythe" was, of course, George Wythe, the famous Virginia jurist and statesman. He, too, must have found the poem amusing. It hardly seems likely that Tucker would have asked him to take the poem to Jodrell otherwise! Tucker also wrote two other mock-English ballads, "The Monks of Waltham Abbey," and "The Fall of Percy." Neither of these is any more readable today than *The Knights and Friars,* and have not been included in this collection.

The year 1786 seems to have marked the beginning and the end of Tucker's interest in imitating the old English ballad. Of the remaining nineteen tales, three are free translations from La Fontaine's *Contes* (Tucker owned a copy), and sixteen are based on incidents that were supposed to happen—or possibly did happen—in Virginia. In fact, eight of these tales bear the notation "a true story." Four of these are in this collection. They are, "Humps and Robin," "The Tobacco-Pipe," "The Faithful Mastiff," and "The Discontented Student."

In 1790, Tucker gathered together several of his tales and began a "Prologue to the Tales," in imitation of Chaucer's prologue to *The Canterbury Tales*. Chaucer, having suffered through an English winter, welcomed the advent of spring, but Tucker, having suffered through a Virginia autumn, welcomes the coming of winter, for that is the season when "autumn's fogs and sickly dews are past," and "youthful lovers"

> No more restrained by fever's dread alarms
> With rapture rush into each other's arms.

Tucker wrote about a dozen character sketches and indicated which tales were to be told by each traveler—*The Knights and Friars* by his doctor, "Jerry Walker" by his miller—but he never completed the project.

These tales and anecdotes not only reveal another facet of Tucker's personality, but they give us a picture of the common round of existence in eighteenth-century Virginia—the dusty road, the inn, the thirsty traveler, the wedding in the home with the guests sleeping on the floor. They remind us that "our founding fathers" loved unpolite "practical" jokes and could laugh at sex. They round out and humanize the one-dimensional picture of our ancestors that history has left us. Like Beverley's remarkable flower, they are "rarities" that would be "unpardonable to omit." And we are no longer so easily embarrassed as Beverley's "grave gentleman!"

Notes

All biographical material about Tucker has been taken from Mary Haldane Coleman, *St. George Tucker, Citizen of No Mean City* (Richmond, 1938). All quotations from Tucker's letters are from those in the Tucker-Coleman Collection, Earl Gregg Swem Library, The College of William and Mary in Virginia.

1. His pathetic story is well told by Lewis Leary, "The Literary Career of Nathaniel Tucker, 1750-1807," *Historical Papers of the*

Trinity College Historical Society, Series XXIX (Durham, 1951).

2. Coleman, p. 28.

3. "Letters of William T. Barry," *William and Mary Quarterly* 13 (1905): 109-110.

4. S. S. Paterson, "The Supreme Court of Appeals of Virginia," *The Green Bag* 5 (1893): 321.

5. *A Dissertation on Slavery, With a Proposal for the Gradual Abolition of it in the State of Virginia* (Philadelphia, 1796; republished in New York, 1861). Tucker's plan for gradual manumission was based on his premise that if the freed slaves were deprived of all civil rights, they would naturally emigrate to unsettled areas (the Southwest) of the continent, where they would set up their own society. When the United States acquired the Louisiana Territory, Tucker suggested it as an area of settlement for the freed slaves.

6. *Reflections on the Policy of Encouraging the Commerce of the Citizens of the United States, and of Granting them Exclusive Privileges in Trade* (Richmond, 1785). Tucker argued that the United States had fought in vain for political independence from Britain unless they had also achieved economic independence. He advocated tariff barriers against Britain, reciprocal trade agreements with certain other countries, and federal and state incentives to American shipbuilders, owners, and operators.

7. *Reflections on the Cessation of Louisiana to the United States* (Washington, 1785). Tucker wrote that the purchase was a bargain on a cost-per-acre basis, and that it dispelled the threat of involvement with France and Britain, since it eliminated contact with them in that area. However, he feared the consequences of a rush on the part of Americans to emigrate there. In this respect, he agreed with Jefferson, who believed that emigrants "should be forbidden to cross the river [the Mississippi] until we shall have filled up all the vacant country on this side" (Henry Nash Smith, *Virgin Land* [Cambridge, Mass., 1950], p. 15).

8. Isaac Weld, *Travels Through the States of North America,*

and the Provinces of Upper and Lower Canada, During the Years 1795, 1796, and 1797 (London, 1807), p. 168.

9. The manuscript is in the Hook Collection, University of Virginia. On the back of the sheet on which the poem is written is the notation, "Found among the papers of Mrs. Dolly Madison after her death."

10. Richard Rush, then comptroller of the Treasury. The letter is quoted in Mrs. George P. Coleman, "Randolph and Tucker Letters," *The Virginia Magazine of History and Biography* 42 (1934): 129.

11. Andrew A. Lipscomb, ed., *The Writings of Jefferson* (Washington, 1904), 12: 252, 327, 389-391.

12. Paul Leicester Ford, ed., *The Writings of Thomas Jefferson* (New York, 1896), 6: 328.

13. Jodrell's copy of Tucker's poem is now in the Yale Collection of American Literature.

THE POEMS

The Tucker House, on Nicholson St., Williamsburg.

POEMS AMONG FRIENDS

Written on Miss Cocke's Wedding Day.

Of all the sprightly girls in town,
In sack, or negligee, or gown,
    Or plain Virginia frock,
There's none that can a charm impart
To captivate a faithful heart
    Like lovely Patsy Cocke.

So graceful is her mien and air,
And then her face is wondrous fair
    The man must be a block,
Who's unsubdued by charms like these,
And makes it not his joy to please
    The lovely Patsy Cocke.

But hark. She speaks: the youthful train
Attentive listening to the strain,
    In crowds around her flock.
So very pungent is your wit
You knock down all you plan to hit
    My charming Patsy Cocke.

Would fate to me this fair one grant,
(If I was out of reach of want)
    I'd take her in her smock:
Content with what my fortune gave
No other riches would I crave
    But thee, my Patsy Cocke.

The mariner, who, tempest tost,
Beholds his laboring vessel lost
    And dashed against a rock,
Never felt such anguish and despair
As I in losing thee, my fair,
    My charming Patsy Cocke.

Jan. 14, 1775

This poem was a work of collaboration with a friend, Dr. James McClurg, who wrote the stanzas marked with asterisks.

The Belles of Williamsburg

Wilt thou, adventurous pen, describe,
The gay, delightful, silken tribe,
    That maddens all our city;
Nor dread, lest while you foolish claim,
A near approach to beauty's flame,
    Icarus' fate may hit ye!*

With singed pinions tumbling down,
The scorn and laughter of the town,
    Thou'lt rue thy daring flight,
While every miss, with cool contempt,
Affronted by the bold attempt,
    Will tittering, view thy plight.*

Yet girls, to you devoted ever,
The object still of our endeavor,
    Is somehow to amuse ye;
And if, instead of higher praise,
You only laugh at these rude lays,
    We'll willing excuse ye.*

Advance then, each illustrious maid,
In order bright, to our parade,
    With beauty's ensigns gay!
And first two nymphs who rural plains
Forsook, disdaining rustic swains,
    And here exert their sway.*

Myrtilla's beauties, who can paint!
The well-turned form, the glowing taint,
    May deck a common creature;
But who can make the expressive soul,
With lively sense inform the whole,
    And light up every feature?*

At church Myrtilla lowly kneels,
No passion but devotion feels,
  No smiles her looks environ;
But let her thoughts to pleasure fly,
The basilisk is in her eye,
  And on her tongue the siren.

Fond youth! no longer gaze—beware,
Lest once enclosed, the dangerous fair,
  May leave you in the lurch:
The god who poets makes his case,
I supplicate, that I may ne'er
  Behold her—but at church.*

More vivid beauty, fresher bloom,
With taints from nature's richest loom,
  In Sylvia's features glow:
Would she Myrtilla's arts apply,
And catch the magic of her eye,
  She'd rule the world below.*

See Laura, sprightly nymph, advance,
Thro' all the mazes of the dance,
  With light, fantastic toe!
See laughter sparkling in her eyes!
At her approach new joys arise,
  New fires within us glow.

 "See laughter sparkling in her eyes": "These two lines were written by a gent-
leman at that time very much enamored of the lady characterized under the name of
Laura, and afterwards married her. Col. Banister"—Tucker.
 Tucker added this note to a draft of the poem: "The characters were generally
ascribed to the following ladies: Myrtilla, Miss Fleming; Sylvia, Miss. S. Fleming;
Laura, Miss Blair; Aspasia, Miss Patsy Digges; Delia, Miss E. Digges; Cordella, Miss
E. Cocke; Artemesia, Miss Taliefro. The town was too good natured to ascribe the
characters of Statira and Melisandra to any particular ladies, so that they are supposed
to be mere fancy pieces."

Such sweetness in her look is seen,
Such brilliant elegance of mien,
     So jaunty and so airy;
Her image in our fancy reigns,
All night she gallops thru' our brains,
     Like little Mab, the fairy.

Aspasia next, with kindred soul,
Disdains the passions that control
     Each gently pleasing art:
Her sportive wit, her frolic lays,
And graceful form attract our praise,
     And steal away the heart.

We see in gentle Delia's face,
Expressed by every melting grace,
     The sweet complacent mind
While hovering round her, soft desires
And hope, gay smiling fan their fires,
     Each shepherd thinks her kind.

The god of love mistook the maid
For his own Psyche, and 'tis said
     He still remains her slave:
And when the boy directs her eyes,
To pierce where every passion lies,
     Not age itself can save!*

With pensive look, and head reclined,
Sweet emblems of the purest mind,
     Lo! where Cordelia sits;
On Dion's image dwells the fair,
Dion, the thunderbolt of war,
     The prince of modern wits!

Not far removed from her side
Statira sits in beauty's pride,
     And rolls about her eyes:
Thrice happy for the unwary heart,
That affection blunts the dart,
     Which from her quiver flies.

Whence does that beam of beauty dawn?
What luster overspreads the lawn?
　　What suns those rays dispense?
From Artemisia's brow they came;
From Artemisia's eyes the flame;
　　That dazzles every sense.

But who is she, whose massy chain
A motley tribe of youths sustain
　　And frisk and dance around her?
Like Cerberus they guard the fair,
With triple clamors fill the air,
　　And with the din confound her.

'Tis Melissandra, matchless fair!
The widowed prey to black despair
　　By Damon's loss oppressed,
Whom neither fond attempts to gain,
Nor antic gambols in her chain
　　Can banish from her breast.

Thrice happy Damon, that you died,
Where sepulture is ne'er denied,
　　To any pious swain!
For if, on this side of the Styx,
You wandered still, such curious tricks
　　Might bring you back again.

At length fatigued with beauty's blaze
The feeble muse no more essays
　　Her picture to complete,
The promised charms of younger girls,
When nature the gay scene unfurls,
　　Some happier bard shall treat.*

1777

1790

41

"The following [two] dreams were written at the wedding of Mr. Nelson and Miss Cary, and were produced for the entertainment of the company each morning when they assembled at breakfast; the ceremony of putting bridecake under the head at night having been previously observed by the whole company."

A Dream on Bridecake

Dear girls, since you the task impose
Of scribbling rhyme, or humbler prose,
Whene'er the bridecake fills the brain
With emblematic dreams of pain,
Or pleasure to be had hereafter,
Or, whatso'er can move your laughter,
The swain to you devoted ever
Will every try his best endeavor,
To tell you in his doggerel strain,
What fancies visited his brain.
    Brimful of claret wine and perry,
You know I went to bed quite merry,
But, as I soon grew wonderous sick,
I wished my carcass at Old Nick.
At length, I sunk into a nap,
With head reclined in fancy's lap;
She rubbed my temples, chaffed my brain,
And then displayed this scene of pain.
    Methought, the claret I'd been drinking
So far from giving aid to thinking,
Had muddled my idea-box,
And clapped my body in the stocks.
Beneath a beach's spreading shade
At lubber's length my limbs were laid;
My tongue alone had power to move,
To rest in vain might wish to rove:
Just then, my Flora passing by
This pretty object chanced to spy;
The wanton saw my hapless case,
And clapped me in a warm embrace;

Her balmy lips to mine she pressed,
And leaned her bosom on my breast,
Her fingers everywhere were gadding,
And set my soul a madding;
Whilst I, in vain, resistance made,
Still on my back supinely laid.
She whispered something in my ear
Which I could not distinctly hear:
Then cried, "Pray when will you be sober?"
"My dear," said I, "not till October.
"My nerves I find are all unstrung
"Except the one that rules my tongue;
"Their wonted tones so wholly lost
"I shan't recover till a frost."
Away the wanton baggage flew
Laughing like any one of you
And left me in that sordid plight,
To mourn the follies of the night.

Sept. 19, 1777

A Second Dream on Bridecake

Well—sure no mortal e'er was cursed
With dreams like mine—for they're the worst
That ever visited a sinner,
E'en after fat turtle dinner,
And six good bottles to defend him
From evils that might else attend him.
    Methought, I turned a mighty rover
Resolved new countries to discover,
And having travelled all around
The globe, a desert isle I found,
Where witches with their train resort
To amuse themselves with magic sport.
    As soon as I set foot on land,

And, in an instant—think how shocking!
Turned me into a white silk stocking,
Then wrapped me up among a dozen
Which she was carrying to a cousin.
Thru' various stores and shops I past,
But got to Williamsburg at last,
Where Flora, to the country gadding
Resolved to buy me for a wedding:
My fate I thought was much improved,
For Flora was the maid I loved;
But, little dreamed of pains in store,
Such as ne'er mortal felt before.
The wedding day at length was come,
The girls retired to a room,
Where first they dizzen out the bride,
That done—they for themselves provide.
My Flora laid me on the bed
Whilst she was dressing out her head;
And little thinking who was near,
She laid her snowy bosom bare,
Then wiped her ivory neck and breast,
And then proceeded with the rest.
      But now, began the dreadful part,
Which plunged a dagger in my heart;
She thrust her hand into my throat,
And quickly turned me, inside out;
Then raised her pretty little foot,
And finding that my mouth would suit,
She drew me quickly on her heel,
Which made my very vitals feel.
But, here methinks I shall disclose
The beauty of her foot and toes;
Her foot and toes were alabaster
And whiter, far, than Paris plaster;
Of mother-pearl I thought her nails
Or else, the silverfish's scales.
She tried to draw me on her leg,
I stuck, and would compassion beg,
But, as, alas, I could not speak,
She forced me on without a squeak.

Her polished knee I next embraced,
And there I stuck until the last;
For tho' she wished to draw me higher,
Yet, troth, I would not venture nigher.
Then to my grief, and great surprise
She with her garter bound my eyes.
Good heaven, was ever such a case?
Was ever man in such a place?
My Flora tripped about, but where
She went, her stocking still was there;
I still embraced her leg and knee,
But yet no object could I see,
Until she went to bed at night,
When she restored me to my sight;
But then, with wonder and surprise,
Poor I, like Milton, lost my eyes;
And thus to utter darkness hurled,
I wished myself in the other world.

Sept. 20, 1777

Christmas Verses for the Printer's Devil, 1784

Now the season for mirth and good eating advances,
Plays, oysters and sheldrakes, balls, mince pies and dances;
Fat pullets, fat turkeys, and fat geese to feed on,
Fat mutton and beef; more by half than you've need on;
Fat pigs and fat hogs, fat cooks and fat venison,
Fat aldermen ready the haunch to lay hands on;
Fat wives and fat daughters, fat husbands and sons,
Fat doctors and parsons, fat lawyers and duns:
What a dancing and fiddling, and gobbling and grunting,
As if Nimrod himself had just come in from hunting!
These all are your comforts—while mine are so small,
I may truly be said to have nothing at all.
I'm a Devil you know, and can't live without fire,
From your doors I can see it, but I dare not come nigher;
Now if you refuse me some wood, or some coal,
I must e'en go and warm, in old Beelzebub's hole;
Next, tho' I'm a devil, I drink and I eat,
Therefore stand in need of some rum, wine and meat;
Some clothes too I want—for I'm blacker than soot,
And a hat, and some shoes, for my horns and my foot;
To supply all these wants, pray good people be civil
And give a few pence to a poor printer's devil.

Dec. 25, 1784

Frances Bland Tucker. From a portrait in the possession of Dr. Janet C. Kimbrough.

Tucker wrote this poem in bed, six days after the death of his wife, Frances.

To Sleep

1

Come gentle Sleep and weigh my eyelids down
And o'er my senses shed oblivion's balm,
'Tis thine alone corroding care to drown,
'Tis thine alone the troubled soul to calm.

2

'Tis thine t'assuage the cruel stings of grief,
And scatter roses o'er a bed of thorns.
From thee alone affliction seeks relief
Even whilst from others that relief she scorns.

3

Thou o'er misfortune throwest thy murky veil
And from our eyes dost kindly hide the past,
Touched by thy poppies memory too shall fail,
And reason bend, like willows with the blast.

4

Thy dreams past happiness can bring again,
And to a dungeon give an Eden's charms;
Pluck from my heart its agonizing pain,
Restore my love—my Fanny to my arms—

5

This bed the scene of all my joys and woes
Awakes Remembrance with her busy train,
Where Bliss unrivalled used to court repose,
Unrivalled Sorrow wakes to endless pain.

6

Dear partner of my blissful hour and care
Friend of my soul, and mistress of my heart
With thee, e'en wretchedness could bliss appear,
Without thee, even blessings yield a smart.

7

Come then O Sleep, on downy pinions come
By dreams attended, hover 'round my head,
Convey my sorrows to the silent tomb
And raise a sleeping angel from the dead.

Jan. 24, 1788

To Mr. Page on His Marriage

Farewell rhyming; farewell writing
    Dodesley, too, a long farewell
Love and Hymen now inviting
    P——must break your magic spell.

Rhyme like Circe's draught bewitching
    I was scribbling day and night
Scratching, thus produced by itching
    Still increases the delight.

Dodesley next my thought engrosses.
    Merchants, thus, by fortune blessed
To secure their wealth from losses
    Lock it, in an iron chest.

Love and Hymen now inviting
    P——must break the magic spell
Farewell rhyming, farewell writing
Dodesley, too, a long farewell.

Mar. 1790

To Mr. Page
On His Marriage to Miss Lowther

Friend of my heart! may this auspicious day
Renew those blessings which you once enjoyed.
Oh! may they ne'er again be snatched away,
Nor e'er thy peace of mind again destroyed.

May all thy sorrows past be like a dream,
From which the troubled sleeper wakes to bliss;
So shall thy past and future blessings seem
But one protracted scene of happiness.

Whate'er of earthly, or of heavenly charms
Adorned thy Fanny's form, or face or mind
When bounteous heaven gave her to thy arms;
On! mays't thou in thy Margarita find.

Thus with each charm and grace and virtue stored,
Which heaven propitious to thy Fanny gave,
In her, thy Fanny's self shall be restored
And e'en on earth shall triumph o'er the grave.

Mar. 27, 1790

Hymn to the Creator

O God! whose word spake into birth,
Whate'er existence boasts;
The moon, the stars, the sun, the earth,
The heavens, and all their hosts.

From world to world from sun to sun,
I turn my wondering eyes;
Their swiftest glance thy works outrun:
New suns and worlds arise!

"thy Fanny's form": Fanny was Page's first wife.
"Margarita": Margaret Lowther.

Thy wonders still my soul pursues
Through each remoter world,
Till sight and thought their aid refuse,
To utter darkness hurled:

There lost—through endless time and space
I seek thy light divine:
O grant me Lord! to see Thy face,
But—let Thy mercy shine.

Jan. 13, 1790

1792

Riddles

1

A pearl in Latin speech shall be my first,
In grammar rules, my next, a bishop versed.
Judah's first born my third will just supply,
Grant me, kind heaven, the whole, or let me die!

Nov. 7, 1789

1790

2

My first a mighty kingdom shall portray,
Where freedom, now triumphant, bears the sway.
The line of beauty as by Hogarth found,
Will lengthen and at once complete the sound.
My next in books—nay more in courts you'll find.
The youthful virgin's form, in all combined;
Whence beams the dawning of an angel's mind.

1790

3

Charade

My first in sultry climates wafts in air
My next from many you may nicely pair,
Two-fifths of night, with just three-fourths of cold
And that which Sarah gained when she was old,
A beauteous virgin's name will straight unfold.

1790

4

Charade

My first devoutly humble met reproof,
In Zion's temple while she stood aloof.
My next to Britain's king a terror grown,
Made many a simple knight of many a drone.
My whole's the picture of my last reversed,
And bears a strong resemblance to my first.

1790

5

To Mrs. Pope

I saw today upon our green,
A thing I have not lately seen,
Although it happens night and day
At balls, at concert, and at play.
But that you may the more applaud,
I'll tell it to you in a charade.
My first at Versailles, or St. James is seen,
When the idol of worship's a king or a queen.
My next in all parts of the ocean is found,
Except where ice-regions prescribe it a bound.
My third is of lasses, and lads the delight,
As witness the Capitol, this very night.

Mar. 6, 1817

Epigrams

1

On July 30, 1791, John Page wrote Tucker, "But now for the epigram I promised in the beginning of the scrawl. It is an impromptu occasioned by Mrs. Page's telling me that Webster in one of his lectures said that the word *wound* was improperly pronounced *woond*, unless applied as in the epigram—for after writing one I ran out the thought as you say I always do in a second, a Peter Pindaric. Take them both here they are:

> When hostile arms assail, and you cry zounds!
> The deep infected strokes you may call wounds.
> But when by gentle glows a lover swoons,
> The critic Webster sounds it woonds.

> When Mars attacks
> With broadsword hacks,
> Each frightful gash that's found
> Is called a ghastly wound.
> When Cupid's darts
> Pierce soft hearts
> The holes they make
> In maid or rake,
> Because these die in swoons
> Webster says we may call "woonds."

Tucker replied with these three epigrams:

> The charge to battle should Bellona sound
> Each well-aimed stroke inflicts a ghastly wound,
> But pierced by Cupid's dart when Streppon swooned,
> Cries critic Webster softly—"What a woond!"

> A battle fought—cries critic Webster "Zounds!
> What blood and slaughter—what disastrous wounds!"
> But pierced by Cupid's dart when Streppon swooned
> He whispers softly—"bless me! what a woond!"

53

Noah Webster's Rule of Pronouncing
Simplified

When Daphne, jilted at her toilet swooned,
No tender heart was sunk with such a wound;
But when she pricked her finger, friends around
Exclaimed with horror; bless us! what a wound!

2

    In another, undated letter, Page wrote, "Mousr. De la Borde was going on a visit to Ferney; Madam du Barry begged of him to give Voltaire two kisses from her. He sent her in return these four lines:

> *Quoi! deux baisers sur la fin de ma vie!*
> *Quel passeport daigner vous m'envoyer!*
> *Ah! c'en est trop, adorable Egerie,*
> *Je serais mort de plaisir au premier.*

Only think of these Verses, when he was almost eighty!"
Page then offered two verse translations of his own:

> Ah, dear Egeria you have given
>   One passport sure too much;
> *One* kiss would send me quick to heaven
>   Of what use then *two such?*

> What! *two* kisses when near my end!
>   What passport have you deigned to give me!
> Ah! too much of it my dear you send
>   The *first* with joy would kill, believe me.

Tucker replied with this one:

> God's! To Elysium what a passport's here!
>   Two kisses by Egeria given!
> The second I shall lose, I fear:
>   Transported by the first to heaven.

Tucker wroter this couplet about his own wedding on October 8, 1791, to Frances Skipwith Carter, and sent it to Frances's sister:

A subject to write a farce on;
All drest so fine! . . . to see the parson.

4

Since its adoption in 1777, the flag had consisted of thirteen stars and thirteen stripes. After Vermont entered the Union in 1791, and Kentucky in 1792, a change was necessitated. On January 13, 1794, Washington signed into law an act that increased the number of stars and stripes to fifteen each. Tucker's epigram, written in February, echoes the same negative attitude toward the Federalist administration that he had expressed the previous year in his Probationary Odes

Columbia's flag displays an emblem bright,
New stripes her lashes mark—new stars her night.

On Reading of Tho Heath's Motion in Congress
to Prohibit the Printing of the Speeches of the Members

Yes, Johnny, thou art surely right
    The Press's freedom to subdue,
For should they print what you indite
    T'would damn the press, as well as you.

On Reading a Ridiculous Encomium on
General Washington

The fool that should a diamond varnish,
Its genuine luster would but tarnish;
So 'tis when fools by flattery aim,
To gild a truly glorious name.

The name of John Adams's birthplace, Braintree (now Quincy), Mass., lent itself to satirical attacks by the anti-Federalists. Tucker wrote this epigram in December, 1797, when Adams was elected president:

> Quoth Jed to Tim, where did our John
>   Such heaps of knowledge gather.
> As if in Paradise he'd been,
>   With Eve—or Satan, rather?
>
> Quoth Tim, I guess that famous tree
>   That once in Eden grew,
> Hath been transplanted to our town,
>   And got a name quite new.
>
> For sure as Latin's learned at college
>   At Braintree John picked up his knowledge.

8

Impromptu, on Seeing the Name of Wilson Curle
Carved in a Corner of the House of Delegates
in Williamsburg, Dated 1776

> Whilst on this floor some rise to deathless fame,
> Curle in the corner sits and carves his name.
>   (Perhaps better thus:)
> Here Henry spoke, and rose to deathless fame:
> Curle in the corner sat, and carved his name.

Written in a County Courthouse

> Here Justice sits and holds her scales:
> But ah! her balance often fails.

On a Young Lady Vain of the Number
of Her Admirers

See beauteous Chloe, followed by a train
Of powdered coxcombs, of their number vain:
If numerous sweethearts constitutes a toast,
Her namesake in the kennel more can boast.

11

Epigram

When Celia dances, 'tis with as much force,
As any racer, straining o'er the course!
Her face, at once, all water and all fire;
If this enflames, that quenches all desire.

12

On the Same

Diana's nymphs returning from the chase
In crystal streams their fervid limbs solace;
But through the dance when lovely Celia flies,
Each friendly pore, a cooling stream supplies.

13

When lovely Sappho on the guitar plays
A gentle rill comes trickling thru' her stays,
Till overwhelmed with exercise and heat
She seems a water nymph; dissolved in sweat.

To William Nelson Esq., of Charles-City

How great your misfortune, dear Will, I can't well say,
In losing our sweet entertainment at Chelsa,
Where Madam Dunbarton had asked us to meet her
And partake of a frolic, I think called sham Peter.
But there was no sham—for we had in reality
The cream of good cheer, with true hospitality.
But first, like old Homer, methinks I should tell
The names of the party that pleased me so well.
Sweet Madam Dunbarton, our hostess, you know,
Whose roses will ever continue to blow;
Who like a ripe peach in the summer, is sweeter,
Than the blossoms of spring,so much praised in meter.
Next Laura the sprightly, so cheerful and gay,
You would swear she was just in the middle of May:
Like Hebe, by time, she no older appears,
For it adds to her charms, as well as her years.
Aunt Betty comes next, who careless, through life
Has past all her days, without being a wife;
And if all her days she could pass o'er again,
I'm persuaded, through choice, she would careless remain.
Our good friends the Doctor and Madam Barraud,
Were both somewhat late in getting abroad.
Our hearts were rejoiced when we saw her appear,
Though rather too late to partake our good cheer.
But as to the Doctor he ate very hearty,
And to tell you the truth was the life of the party.
Fanny Currie, Miss Dawson, Miss Farley and Fan,
With my Godson I— C— that pretty young man,
Messieurs W— and B—, Adonises Twain,
In the eyes of the lasses who dance on the plain,
With Madame, and myself, though last not the least,
In my love and affection attended the feast.
Three chariots, together, in order proceed,
To these on gay horses our gallants succeed;
Whilst the hearts of the lasses did terribly flutter,
'Twixt thinking of them, and Madame's bread and butter.
Arrived, in the orchard a carpet we found,
That was spread to prevent any damps from the ground,
While the fruit on the trees hung in clusters around.

A table with teacups and saucers was spread,
When presently entered the butter and bread.
The last like a sponge—the butter so nice,
Like a marigold yellow, was covered with ice.
Apoquimini cakes, with a delicate shad,
Cold ham and broiled chicken, the best to be had,
All seasoned with mirth and good humor unfeigned
So keen were our stomachs as well as our wits
That we dwelt a long while on the savory bits;
Then with sherbert and negus the banquet was crowned
Whilst the toast and the sentiment gaily went 'round.
Till perceiving the approach of the heat of the day,
We reluctantly parted, and all drove away,
And made such a rout, as we entered the town
You would almost have thought that the college fell down.

July 9, 1795

To Miss Fanny Currie

No language, dear Fanny, can tell you the rout
That in sweet little Williamsburg lately fell out,
Occasioned, good luck! by the wonderful news,
Of a cargo of ribbons, and gauzes, and shoes.
Miss C— who the first the glad tidings received
Out of breath ran to tell, but was scarcely believed
By Mrs. B— and sweet Nancy Taylor,
Who skipped topmast high, as alert as a sailor;
Away then they posted to get the first sight
Which put Mrs. Charlton in such a sad fright
She slammed to the door of her shop in their faces.
Madam T— and Dunbar who were taking a ride
The throng at the door no sooner espied,
Than they called out to Robin to stop, and jumped out,
Like rats from their holes, when they're out to the rout.
The bellman at length was sent all through the town,
To proclaim that tomorrow the sight would be shown,
So the ladies all homeward reluctantly sent,
To wait till the night intervening was spent.

Some resolved to rise early, and some to sit up,
And to keep them awake took a cheerupping cup.
Madam T— went to bed, but her brain was so warm,
She tumbled and tossed like a ship in a storm.
At midnight at length she got up and was dressed,
Ere her drowsy dull husband had turned in his nest.
The morning star rose, but the horns of day,
Were supposed to have strayed: for you could not well see,
When Robin for once more alert than Apollo,
Cried gee-up to his horses, and bade Ned to follow.
The chariot had scarcely arrived at the gate
When Madame cried out she no longer could wait;
Fan, Betsy, and Polly came clattering downstairs,
Rushed out and jumped into the chariot by pairs.
Away then they drove to the eastward to chide
The dull god of day who was still with his bride
Though some have supposed that he had an intrigue
With good Mrs. Ch—n, and both were in league
To wear out the patience of those at the door.
Till at length Mrs. Charlton and Phoebus once more
Op'ed the gates of the morning and eke of the store.
In rushed all the crowd, but to paint you this scene
Would require the pencil of Hogarth I ween,
One snatched up a shoe, and another its fellow.
"What a sweet pretty ribbon! These colors, how mellow!"
"This muslin's so lovely— This feather's quite killing."
"Pray look at this fan— Two sweet doves a billing."
"I shall die if I don't get this hat and this feather."
"Ma'am, I chose them first."—"No, Ma'am, not so neither;
I fixed my eyes on them the moment I entered."
"Ma'am, I got in first or I should not have ventured."
"See this beautiful doll—such eyes and such hair!
She seems to want only one thing, I declare."
The sun now was up, and Myrtilla was called,
But the jade seemed the deafer the louder I bawled,
"Pray where is your Mistress, and where are my keys?
Go bring me some water to shave if you please;
And bid them make haste with the breakfast d'ye hear,
I'm half dead with waking all night I declare."
"Sir, Mistress is gone with the keys in her pocket,
In the drawer lie your razors, I cannot unlock it.

The breakfast is ready, and all on the spot
But the coffee and tea, which Mistress forgot.''
So away to Dunbarton I posted in haste,
Resolved of their breakfast to get a small taste.
When instantly up drove man Robin with Ned:
''Ma'am, Mistress has sent—'' ''Robin what's that you said?
Get my cloak, and my shawl and my clogs; I protest
I can't eat a morsel.'' ''Indeed, Ma'am, you'd best.''
''No, no my dear Becky—Come, Molly, let's go.''
Aunt Becky and I were thus left all alone
With the coffee, and tea, and a sweet bacon bone;
And you well may believe that we both took a slice,
Of the butter and bread that were equally nice.
        Now Phoebus had finished one-half of his career,
When slowly we saw the old chariot appear
Not the famed Trojan Horse with the Greeks in his belly,
Proceeded more heavily on let me tell ye.
Band-boxes and bundles were stuffed in the front,
You'd have thought that the seat had nobody upon't;
But wedged in one corner, at length I descried
Sweet Madam Dunbar, and Madam t'other side.
The door then bounced open and poor little Poll,
From under the seat crept with Bet and her doll.
The whole were half-smothered and puffing and blowing.
''My dear husband, I'm starved, I'm dead, I'm agoing.
Some breakfast in pity I pray you bestow,
Indeed, I shall faint if you answer me no.
See this hat, and these shoes, and this feather so nice,
And this beautiful fan— What a charming device!
This sweet little doll with her lovely blue eyes,
Is Madam Dunbar's—I declare 'twould surprise
You to hear all the various remarks that were made
By the ladies upon't—from her toes to her head.
Come Aleck, the coffee—ladies, pray take a seat
How charming this coffee! this butter, how sweet!
O that beautiful doll! That hat and that feather!
See there now come Fanny and Molly together.
O there is Mrs. Banister just going home;
She promised to dine here; I hope she won't come.

Let me die if I know what to have for our dinner
Phill, pray look about you and get us some fish,
I protest I don't know what to do for a dish.
Five guineas, my husband, see here is the bill,
Is all I have spent. You must, and you will
I am sure find the money to pay off this score;
'Tis the devil you know to be, and seem poor."
     So you see, my dear Fanny, how things here have passed,
The husband poor soul, pays the piper at last.

Mar. 27, 1796

     "This little piece has reference to a most beautiful picture at
Bishop Madison's, where a lady is represented with a child in her
lap, in the most bewitching attitude. The question was archly pro-
posed by a young lady who might have sat for the picture." *The lady
was Miss Nancy Taylor*.

To Cynthia

When Cynthia's crescent I behold
A luster shedding 'round her brow,
I'm half convinced when I am told,
That Art can vie with Nature, now.

But when her beauteous eyes I view,
That sparkle with a ray divine,
I feel the ancient maxim's true,
That Art cannot, like Nature, shine.

O! Were I suffered to descry
Those other orbs that swell below,
Where fancy sets before my eye,
Two rosebuds, peeping through the snow;
Transported at the sight, I'd swear,
Art ne'er can rival Nature, there.

Then Cynthia, deign to smile upon
And make me, thy Endymion.

Mar. 10; 1799

Resignation

Days of my youth! Ye have glided away;
Locks of my youth! Ye are frosted and gray;
Eyes of my youth! Your keen sight is no more;
Cheeks of my youth! Ye are furrowed all o'er;
Strength of my youth! All your vigor is gone;
Thoughts of my youth! Your gay visions are flown!

Days of my youth, I wish not your recall;
Locks of my youth, I'm content ye shall fall;
Eyes of my youth, ye much evil have seen;
Cheeks of my youth, bathed in tears have ye been;
Thoughts of my youth, ye have led me astray;
Strength of my youth; why lament your decay!

Days of my age! Ye will shortly be past;
Pains of my age, but a while can ye last;
Joys of my age, in true wisdom delight;
Eyes of my age, be religion your light;
Thoughts of my age, dread ye not the cold sod;
Hopes of my age, be ye fixed on your God!

Mar. 21, 1807

Burletta

"Composed partly between sleeping and waking in the morning; June 10th, 1807."

With lungs loud as Stentor's,
I'll sing my tormentors,
More frightful than centaurs;
And him that adventures,
To slay my tormentors;
    And him that adventures
To slay my tormentors,
       And him that adventures,
       To slay my tormentors,
          To slay my tormentors
          To slay my tormentors.

See they rush to to my bed:
How they fill me with dread!
Hovering over my head,
Like the ghosts of the dead,
Which a charnel o'erspread!
    Like the ghosts of the dead,
    Which a charnel o'erspread!
       Which a charnel o'erspread
       Which a charnel o'erspread.

Chorus

With lungs loud as Stentor's
I'll sing my tormentors,
More frightful than centaurs;
And him that adventures,
To slay my tormentors;
    And him that adventures
To slay my tormentors,
       And him that adventures,
       To slay my tormentors
          To slay my tormentors.

See their hosts how they rise!
How they darken the skies!
Oh! they put out my eyes!
Ah! pity my cries!
A plague on these flies!
    Ah! pity my cries!
    A plague on these flies!
      Ah pity my cries!
      A curse on these flies!
        A curse on these flies!
        A curse on these flies!

Chorus

With lungs loud as Stentor's
I'll sing my tormentor's
More frightful than centaurs;
And him that adventures,
To slay my tormentors,
    And him that adventures
    To slay my tormentors
      And him that adventures,
      To slay my tormentors
        To slay my tormentors
        To slay my tormentors.

Song
Tune—A cobbler there was, etc.

I envy no man for his purse, or his wife,
Or his horses, or coach, or his station in life;
With a little content, independence I prize,
And he that seeks more, is more greedy than wise,
    Derry down, etc.

I care not a farthing for term, or vacation;
Or the meeting of Congress to settle the nation;
Or assemblies that talk of divorces and banks,
Pass censures on some, and to others give thanks,
                    Derry down, etc.

What care I, whether Jackson's a general or judge?
Whether Peter or Dabney the circuit shall trudge?
Whether substitutes offered by Mercer or Leigh,
The majority gain is no matter to me.
                    Derry down, etc.

Still less do I care, whether Caesar, or Kate,
Who their freedom have bought, shall remain in the state.
If a street be too wide, or a lane be too close,
Or three pence be given for killing of crows,
                    Derry down, etc.

Speculators, and smugglers, and gamesters and racers,
Now mounted in garrets, now mounted on pacers!
Let who will win the race! whether Blacky or Roan,
Break his rider's neck first, and then break his own.
                    Derry down, etc.

As for demagogues, Federalists, aristocrats,
Now roaring like lions, now purring like cats,
Catterwalling, and scratching, or watching a mouse,
I regard them no more than a flea, or a louse.
                    Derry down, etc.

For the maniac George, and the tyrant of France,
I would they were thrown in a thousand-year's trance;
When waking, well purged of their infamous crimes,
They may turn harmless poets, like me, and make rhymes.
                    Derry down, etc.

Feb. 1812

To Mrs. Page

When a tyrant complains
Of a forger of chains
What mortal believes him sincere!
Since we know 'tis his trade
To make others afraid,
And chains to impose—not to wear.

When a master of arts
To his pupil imparts
A science he thoroughly knows;
How grateful the youth
To the teacher of truth,
For what he so kindly bestows?

In you Madam Page,
The tyrant and sage,
As in Pericles, seem to unite.
'Gainst chains while you preach
Your fair pupil to teach,
That art, in which all must delight.

Dec. 10, 1812

The Sick Man's Return for a Kiss

The grateful heart that can't repay
The favors it has prized,
Shall find acceptance in that day
When hearts are undisguised—

The widow's mite acceptance found
Where talents were disdained,
The will, and not the offering, crowned
The preference it gained—

While some good folks about us live,
I'm beggared by your kiss,
Accept then all I now can give,
A lovely peach—and *This*——

[Mrs. Page:

Poor feverish soul! You are vastly demure
God grant you a speedy and radical cure
Your return for my kiss I greatly admire
And take the will for the deed as the case doth require.]

A Fable

I dreamed last night, the debt of nature paid,
I, cheek by jowl, was by a Negro laid;
Provoked at such a neighborhood, I cried,
"Rascal! begone. Rot farther from my side."
"Rascal!" said he, with arrogance extreme,
"Thou are the only rascal here, I deem;
Know fallen tyrant, I'm no more thy slave!
Quaco's a monarch's equal, in the grave."

Dec. 25, 1812

"A Fable": "In imitation of one in Bougier's French grammar, by La Fontaine, as well as I recollect: *Je songais cette nuit, que d'envie consumé / Cote a cotes d'un pauvre on m'avait enhumé"* —Tucker.

The Reflections of a Man in His Grand Climacteric

'Tis a folly for Age to repine at the loss
Of the things which it ne'er can again come across;
Agility, strength, youth, and health, are all gone,
And with them the spirits that moved them are flown.

Sad Remembrance must now the enjoyment supply
Of the pleasures that sparkled in Passion's bright eye,
When Youth held the torch, and Hope pointed to bliss,
To be found in a bumper, the dance, or a kiss.

The delusion is past, and diseases and pain
Of vain promised pleasures usurp the domain;
Dull Patience alone can a plaster apply,
Their pangs to assuage till the time comes to die.

That time now approaches, —and Death wields her dart,
And the victim beholds it, well aimed at his heart;
What now shall support him? A life that's well past!
For a conscience that's sound, is a shield to the last.

Then, shall Hope not desert him: that friend of his youth
Shall in age be his nurse, and the teacher of truth:
As she bends o'er his pillow bright visions shall rise,
Whilst to life everlasting she points in the skies.

Aug. 19, 1813. *Aet.* 62

Lines, Supposed to Have Been Found
Upon the Palace Green at Williamsburg
On May Day, 1816

O! what a pleasure's in the town,
To the world, how little known!
    Pleasures, which there is no telling:
Pleasures, which there is no knowing!
When the belles are off, a-beau-ing,
    And the beaus are off a-belle-ing.

O! the sweet, bewitching scene,
Palace grounds, or college green,
    When the beaus, and belles, assembling;
Beaus, their secret thoughts confiding;
Belles, their smiles, and blushes hiding,
    Frowns, and careless looks dissembling.

O! the dear enchanting sight,
When at parties, just at night,
    Beaus, and belles, in pairs advancing;
Beaus their willing partners handing,
Beaus and belles on tiptoe standing,
    Music striking, all a-dancing!

O! how charming in the church!
Beaus and belles in gallery perch;
    As to hear a reverend preacher:
Beaus and belles their eyes a-keeping
Beaus through veils, and fans, a-peeping;
    Little love the only teacher!

May, 1816

Occasioned by Some Remarks on the Word "Prancing," in the Preceding by Three Scrupulous Ladies

Three prudes, a poet's work perusing,
Begun, at once, his rhymes abusing:
"Sure, 'tis enough, for girls to dance!
But here, this poet makes them *prance;*
Like actresses, arrived from France!"
"Deliver us from such wretched stuff;
Sir, write no more: —we've read enough."
    The poet hangs his head awhile,
    Looks up, then answers with a smile:
"Ladies! your criticism's just:
I'll change the phrase: I will: I must!
For who, that ever had a glance
At your bright eyes, ere saw them *prance!*
Though even now, I see them dance."
    A smile, at once, lights up their faces,
    And now, the prudes are changed to graces.

May, 1816

Bacchanalian

I have heard from my youth,
That in wine there is truth:
    And let him who the maxim disputes
Just put by his glass,
And go feed upon grass,
    And drink puddle water with brutes.

Wine renders the sage
Blithe as youth, just of age,
    And as wise as the sage makes the youth,
Whilst together they reel,
And in unison feel,
    That wine is the essence of truth.

71

'Twas by nectar the gods
Held o'er mortals their rods,
　　Much more than the thunder of Jove;
'Twas Falernian wine
Did fair Venus enshrine,
　　And proclaim her the goddess of love.

With imperial tokay,
An empire I'd sway,
　　Far better than Caesar, or Bony;
And with sweet jack, and sherry,
Like Falstaff make merry,
　　And Pegasus mount like a pony.

Wine shows in the glass,
All the charms of the lass
　　That the love-smitten shepherd adores;
And each drop that he sips,
Like the dew on her lips,
　　In his heart a new ecstasy pours.

In the sparkling champagne
He encounters again
　　The sparkles that beam from her eyes;
Like her breath the old hock,
From the true convent stock,
　　An ambrosial odor supplies.

In Madeira he'll find
The attractions that bind
　　His heart, to the heart of the fair;
And in Burgundy trace
The sweet blush of her face,
　　When his passion she heard him declare.

A bumper then fill,
But a drop do not spill,
　　To the lass that each heart can beguile;
Who, like wine, inspires,
Gay hope, love, and fires,
　　And banishes care with a smile.

Apr. 1, 1817

Be Merry and Wise

Of all the enjoyments on earth that we prize
Be mine the choice gift, to be merry, and wise;
Mirth enlivens the heart, and the blood in each vein,
'Tis the province of wisdom excess can restrain.

Mirth delights in the bottle, and smiles on the glass,
And invites to the arms of the love-breathing lass:
While wisdom, with caution a bumper declines,
And love with the chaplet of Hymen entwines.

Mirth and wisdom united will drive away care,
And an antidote prove to remorse and despair;
Then, of all the enjoyments on earth that we prize,
Be mine the choice gift to be merry and wise.

June 8, 1817

Anacreontic

Come fill your glass! to Chloe's eyes,
    This bumper is addressed;
Another to her lips we'll fill
    And two more, to her breast.

Two more we'll fill up to her heart:
    They're not enough! two more!!
And if she has a sweeter part,
    To that, we'll fill a score!

On Mrs. Lucy Nelson (the General's Widow) Attending the Communion Table at Church on a very Cold Day

Though cold the day, yon aged breast
  Is warm with pious zeal:
Though blind those eyes, religion's light
  The Christian still can feel.

A life in virtuous actions spent,
  Its sacred influence shows;
And pious hopes with age increase,
  Like wheat beneath the snows.

Nor doubt it will, in God's good time,
  A heavenly harvest yield,
Abundant, as the fruits of Nile,
  To Pharoah's dreams revealed.

Jan. 4, 1818

Woman

Woman parent of mankind
  Tender nurse of infant years,
Comfort of the sick and blind,
  Soother of all human cares.

Object dear of infant love
  Magnet of the youthful heart,
Every passion born to move,
  Every blessing to impart.

Consort sweet of riper years,
  Idol of the manly breast,
Age's guide through vales of tears,
  To the mansions of the blessed.

Be thou still, as from the first,
    Joy and comfort of my heart,
And when death thy bands shall burst
    May we meet, no more to part.

Sept. 11, 1819

Written on Christmas Day, 1820

All hail, auspicious day!
    When gracious Christ was born;
To point to heaven the way,
    And comfort the forlorn:

To teach frail man to serve,
    And love his God, above;
Nor from that path to swerve:
    His neighbors, next, to love:

The wretched to relieve,
    The humble to exalt,
To comfort those that grieve,
    And to forgive each fault:

The orphan child to breed,
    To clothe the naked poor,
The hungry wretch to feed,
    Nor, drive him from the door:

In all his dealings just;
    His labors for the best:
In God to put his trust;
    And leave to Him the rest.

Dec. 25, 1820

SATIRES

The Alarm
A Real Story Which Happened in Bermuda, in the Year 1776

When first the laurels 'gan to grow
On Admiral Hopkins' dreadful brow,
His fame was o'er the Atlantic spread,
And stoutest bosoms filled with dread.
For governors and folks of state
Were surest objects of his hate;
Thus when to Providence he went,
With cannon he was not content,
But added to his vast renown,
By carrying off the governor Bruere.

On mischief bent, and fraught with guile
Fame hied her to Bermuda's isle.
And in the shape of Afric's son,
Her flight directed to the town.
The hero's feats, his matchless fame
She trumpets forth with loud acclaim,
And adds, that with a mighty train
Of ships he ploughed the watery main,
Whose rapid course was hither bent,
To glut the warrior's fell intent.
"E'en now, borne by the western gales,
I saw," she cried, "his swelling sails,
With other numerous ships beside,
Which o'er the billows proudly ride;
So swift their course, that e'en the sun
Shall set, each wight will be undone."

"The Alarm": In a note to the poem, Tucker explains that "The Governor had that day invited some refugees from Norfolk and his Tory friends to a turtle feast which was interrupted as mentioned in the sequel, by a report spread by a negro that Hopkins had arrived at the west end of the island."

"Admiral Hopkins": Esek Hopkins (1718-1802), commander-in-chief of the fleet of the United States.

"Providence": New Providence, Bahamas.

"carrying off Governor Bruere": Hopkins took Bruere back to the United States in March, 1776.

A general panic now prevails
And every Tory breast assails
With hideous fears—each doughty Whig
Now struts with self-importance big.
Some to the caverned mansions hie;
Some mount the hills, the fleet to spy;
Another train with busy care
For flight with their effects prepare.

It chanced that day was marked by fete
For Dromis to give a treat,
Of turtle to a chosen few
Whose hearts were loyal, warm and true.
Each dainty that the isles afford.
And richest viands crowned the board.
The guests were all conducted in;
Each with his napkin at his chin,
Views with anticipating glee,
The savory stew, and calipee:
With brandished knives they now prepare
To feast upon the dainty cheer;
But as each hand its treasure reared,
The dreadful trump of Fame was heard.
Aghast, they listen to the sound:
Not e'en the Gorgon's hissing head
Could fill their souls with greater dread.
With hairs erect, in wild dismay,
They know not where to bend their way;
Winged by their fears, at length they fly
With sails and oars the bark to ply;
And thus (as mice desert their cheese
If they but hear the sound of keys)
The loyal friends, with panic stored,
The turtle left upon the board.

Written in Bermuda, June, 1776

Parody

By Charles, by title, Lord Cornwallis
The scourge of all rebellious follies,
Lieutenant-general commanding
The British forces of long standing
With those et ceteras at the end
Which mean more than you understand

"Parody": Tucker's note explains that "This doggerel was written in camp, March 20th, 1781." This was five days after the battle of Guilford Courthouse. The British forces, under the command of General Cornwallis, lost twice as many men as the Americans but, because the militia was routed, Cornwallis considered it a British victory and issued the following announcement:

"By the Right Honourable Charles Earl Cornwallis, Lieutenant-general of his Majesty's forces, &c. / A PROCLAMATION. / Whereas, by the blessing of Almighty God, his Majesty's arms have been crowned with signal success, by the complete victory obtained over the rebel forces on the 15th instant, I have thought proper to issue this proclamation to call upon all loyal subjects to stand forth, and take an active part in restoring good order and government. And whereas it has been represented to me, that many persons in this province, who have taken a share in the unnatural rebellion, but having experienced the oppressions and injustice of the rebel government, and having seen the errors into which they have been deluded by falsehoods and misrepresentation, are sincerely desirous of returning to their duty and allegiance, I do hereby notify and promise to all such persons (murderers excepted), that if they will surrender themselves, with their arms and ammunition, at head quarters, or the officer commanding contiguous to their respective places of residence, on or before the 20th of April next, they shall be permitted to return to their homes, upon giving a military parole, and shall be protected in their persons and properties from all sort of violence from the British troops, and will be restored as soon as possible to the privileges of legal and constitutional government. / Given under my hand at headquarters this 18th day of March, A.D. 1781, and in the twenty-first year of His Majesty's reign. / CORNWALLIS." From Lt. Col. Tarleton, *A History of the Campaigns of 1780 and 1781, in the Southern Provinces of North America* (Dublin, 1787).

A Proclamation

Whereas by Providence divine
Which on our arms has deigned to shine
On Thursday last we fought a battle
With lousy, vile, rebellious cattle,
And, to our everlasting glory
(Unaided by a single Tory)
The rebel forces did defeat
And gain a victory complete,
Whereby His Majesty's command
Is reestablished in the land,
And Loyalty uprears its head
While cursed Rebellion goes to bed;
I, therefore, willing to uphold
The weak and to reward the bold,
Do issue this my Proclamation
Without regard to sect or nation.
Requiring every loyal Tory
To come to me and share the glory
And toil of bringing back to reason
The wretches guilty of high treason.
Whereby the government benign
Of Britain's Majesty divine
With luster primitive may shine.
Moreover, since I understand
That divers persons in the land,
By vile seducers led astray
Have left the true and perfect way
Which loyal subjects should pursue
And joined with the rebellious crew,
Grown sorry for their former fault,
Are anxious now to make a halt,
And, cured of their rebellious pride
Would wish to turn to our side,
To such, I hereby notify
(As God will judge me when I die)
That (murderers alone excepted
For whom no grace can be expected),
If they will to my quarters run
With their accoutrements and gun,

In thirty days, next from this date
They shall eschew a rebel's fate,
And be permitted to go back
With a parole, like pill of quack,
To cure the numerous disorders
That rage upon our army's borders;
Or, like a talisman to charm
Our soldiery from doing harm,
Tho' truth obliges us to own
They will not cure a broken bone,
Nor 'gainst the rebels yield assistance
Or keep their army at a distance;
If such effects they could produce
We'd keep them for our army's use.
But this is only by the bye;
On their effects you may rely.

    Let no ill-natured imputation
Be cast on this Proclamation,
Because from hence with God's permission
I mean to march with expedition,
Tho' I confess we do not mean
To go in quest of Mr. Greene,
Who two miles distant, it is said
Weeps o'er his wounds and broken head.
Humanity, the soldier's glory
Which dignifies each loyal Tory,
Which fills each generous Briton's heart
In all my actions stands confessed.
Her voice forbade me to pursue
The frightened, naked, rebel crew
Who filed an half a mile or more
Before their panic they got o'er,
Humanity alike commands
Of bloody deeds to wash our hands,
And should we follow Mr. Greene
Much blood might then be spilt I ween:

"Mr. Green": General Greene, the commander of the American troops at the battle of Guilford Courthouse.

Humanity commands to yield
The wounded whom we won in field,
Nay more she bids us leave behind
The maimed, the halt, the sick, the blind
Among our soldiers who might prove
A hindrance as we backward move.
Her high behests we then obey;
Now strike our tents and march away.
March the eighteenth, eighty-one
At Guilford Courthouse this is done.

Mar. 20, 1781

THE PROBATIONARY ODES

A Dedicatory Ode
To a Would-be Great Man

Jonathan sheweth his profound skill in heraldry—maketh an essay upon the subject of titles, and proposeth a most apt one for a certain distinguished personage.

Ætavis Edite! Hor.

O Thou! whatever be thy title loved,
King of the Romans, Caesar, Czarowitz,
Dauphin, or Prince of Wales, if more approved,
Infant, or Daddy-Vice, as best befits,
Deign from my hands t'accept this savory sprig
To greet thy nostrils, or adorn thy wig.

Say, who can rival thine illustrious line,
Great son of unborn Adam's first-born son,
By right of primogeniture divine
Heir to those titles thy great grandshire won:
Heir to this whole terraqueous globe, no doubt,
As any herald's office can make out.

But since thine humble nature condescends
To wave thy title to the world at large,
Were mine the envied task, the grateful charge,
Thou should'st be greater in my verse sublime
Than e'er was Gog, or Magog yet in rhyme.

"The Probationary Odes": The text of *The Probationary Odes of Jonathan Pindar* printed here is that of the edition published by Bache, in Philadelphia, in 1796. Dates of composition are from Tucker's manuscripts. Except for "A Dedicatory Ode," all of the poems in Part I were printed in Freneau's *National Gazette* on the dates given at the bottom right of the poems. Notes which are not mine are placed within quotes,, followed by "Editor," meaning either Bache or William Branch Giles. They were printed in the book but not in the newspaper.

"To a Would-be Great Man": Vice-President John Adams.

Caesars of old, were by adoption named,
As kings of Romas are by fiction, now;
Hence each securely the succession claimed;
From portents sure, I ween, so wilt not thou;
As gibbet-climbing worthies to the top
Do never rise, but just beneath it drop.

If Dauphin I should hail thee, some would say
I meant to threaten with the guillotine;
If Prince of Wales; —it might a thought betray
Thy dad a madman was, thy dam a queen;
If Czarowitz I style thee; —they would swear,
I meant thy father was a Russian bear.

Infants, in Spain, or Lisbon, may be born
With bears, and bellies round, for ought I know;
With wigs their nappers too they may adorn,
Big as a bushel, and as white as snow:
There, Doctor Slop might for an Infant pass,
So may'st thou there; but not here, by the mass.

Though Congress once, their ignorance to hide,
Forebore on splendid titles to descant,
A partisan who combats on thy side,
A title fitting would not let thee want.
Old George, he swore, might without title shine,
But, most superfluous highness, should be thine.

Ode I
To All the Great Folks in a Lump

The humble petition of Jonathan; containing after the manner of other candidates for honors and offices, many fair promises, which peradventure may never be fulfilled.

Confedere duces, et vulgi stante corona
Surgit ad hos Jonathan. Ovid.

So please your Worships, Honors, Lordships, Graces!
I Jonathan, to Peter Pindar cousin,
Hearing that you possess a mint of places
Have come to ask for less than half a dozen.

I ask not that to serve me you should quit
Your lofty stations or turn out your friends:
No—I've more conscience! and at once admit
Your duty's to consult on means and ends.

Those ends once answered—and the means obtained,
To Jonathan's petition lend an ear:
Nor think his young ambition overstrained,
Head of Department, should his claim appear.

"Ode I": "The practice of both branches of the Legislature, to refer every subject to the head of a department, before they act on it themselves, seems here referred to. But it is not impossible that Jonathan considers the ends of some great folks in getting into office, to have been the more effectually to secure the means of further advantages" (Editor).

84

Heads of Departments, we have seen, can jump
At once into the mysteries of their art:
Not Richmond's Duke excels great K-x the plump,
Not Law to H——n could teach his part.

I ask not dollars; though in truth a few
Would jingle sweetly in a poet's purse:
And since t'encourage arts belongs to you,
A pension would not make the thing the worse.

I ask not such a patronage as brings
To brother heads an influence far and wide;
Commissions, loans, douceurs, jobs, pretty things,
Bank votes, directorships, and offices beside.

Let others, patrons—Me, your client be:
I have abundant zeal, and long to show it;
To celebrate your praises make me free
And dub me here, at once, your laureate Poet.

I'll puff you to the clouds! and, by the pigs,
Whilst there is brightest arch the rainbow spreads,
Comets shall lend their tails to make you wigs.
And powdered sunbeams glitter on your heads.

"Richmond's Duke": "Formerly master-general of the ordinance, and famous for his fortifications for the defense of England against invasions" (Editor).

"K—x": Henry Knox, secretary of war.

"Law": John Law (1671-1729). "Author of the South Sea and Mississippi schemes in England and France" (Editor).

"H—n": Alexander Hamilton, secretary of the Treasury.

"could teach his part": "I am somewhat inclined to doubt whether the sense of this line was not mistaken by Mr. Freneau: the word *could*, I suspect, should have been written *can*. I grant that if the allusion be simply to the famous Mr. Law, *could* would be the proper word. But surely, those who recollect the scrutiny made into the conduct of the late Secretary of the Treasury, will be persuaded that we ought to read, 'Not Law to H—n *can* teach his part' " (Editor).

"It is contended by the Secretary of the Treasury, in his Report on Manufactures, that whilst the 'general welfare' is the object, the public money may be applied, and of course the people taxed to raise it, for every possible object, which in the discretion of Congress may be deemed conducive to the end" (Editor).

I'll swear to all the world—you never dipped
In speculators' kennel your pure hands;
That not a soul of you e'er dealt in script:
To prove my words your broker ready stands.

I'll say—that bank directors though you are,
No private interest ever sways your vote:
That you are chose, just to see all fair,
And, who shall win or lose, care not a groat.

I'll swear—that nation's debt's a blessing vast
Which far and wide its genial influence sheds,
From whence Pactolian showers descends so fast
On theirs—*id est*—the speculators' heads.

That to increase this blessing and entail
To future times its influence benign,
New loans from foreign nations cannot fail,
Whilst standing armies clinch the grand design.

That taxes are not burthens to the rich;
That—they alone to labor drive the Poor;
The lazy rogues would neither plough, nor ditch
Unless to keep the sheriff from the door.

I'll swear—your honors are not like the boy,
Who killed his goose which golden eggs did lay;
Your goose you've no intention to destroy;
Content to squeeze out half a dozen a day.

I'll swear—in treaties you never had a thought
To give up gratis all right of preemption:
Or that you had an agent on the spot,
To purchase for yourselves, I will not mention.

"Bank directors": "It is the prevailing opinion in Philadelphia, that the office of bank director, turned to the best account, is worth 5000 per annum" (Editor).

"nation's debt a blessing": "In the report of the Secretary of the Treasury upon manufactures, as well as in that upon the subject of the public debt, he contends it is a happy thing for the country they are indebted, since it adds so much to the national wealth" (Editor).

"to increase this blessing": "The irredeemable quality of the debt" (Editor).

86

I'll say—that you're well read, and well expound,
Much better than Vattel! the Law of Nations:
That no newfangled doctrines have you found
To fritter states away to corporations.

I'll swear—they owe their charters to your grant,
And if beyond their proper bounds you catch 'em,
The means to bring them back you will not want,
But instant, with a *quo warranto* match 'em.

These things and many more—you'll not disown,
Prove I can flatter in a proper way;
Suppose me now a speculator grown,
Hear what to little Atlas I could say.

June 1, 1793

"To fritter states away": "Said to be insisted on in the arguments of Mr. Chief Justice Jay and Judge Wilson in their decision making states amenable to the judgements of a federal court" (Editor).

Ode II
To Atlas

Jonathan, turned Speculator, in behalf of the whole corps addresseth their great benefactor and patron.

Ingreditor folo, et caput inter nubila condit, Virg. ————*Nunquam dimoveas!* Hor.

Whilst you, great Atlas! prop the State,
Nor totter underneath a weight,
    That would a giant crush;
Let pigmy wights, in Congress Hall,
Set sparrow traps to work your fall,
    Regard them not a rush!

A lion should a spaniel bay,
The king of beasts would keep his way
    Nor heed the babbler's throat;
Then deign not, Atlas, to look down
Or punish with a single frown
    The angry snarler's note.

Whilst on your paper throne you sit
With solid gold beneath your feet
    Fear not a regicide!
Your faithful Janizaries all
Shall muster thick in Congress Hall
    To guard their leader's side.
Go on, great chief, to make us all,
Not from your shoulders cast the ball,
    Lest we, like worms, should drop,
Who on a golden pippin prey,
Till haply on some stormy day
    'Tis shaken from the top.

June 5, 1793

"Atlas": Alexander Hamilton, secretary of the treasury.

Ode III
To a Select Body of Great Men

Jonathan approacheth the holy of holies: —is frightened out of his
senses, and knocked down; —endeavors to deprecate the wrath of of-
fended dignity.

—————————————"Horrisono stridentes cardono facrae
Panduntur portaie."

My Lords! your Poet Laureate, humbly knocks;
And begs permission to approach your door;
Nay! good my Lords! don't set me in the stocks!
I vow to God, that I'll do so no more.

Good Mister Sargeant! spare me this one time!
Lord, Sir! you need not thus have knocked me down!
Wretch that I am! —I'll freely own my crime
Deserves I should be whipped through all the town.

I never said, in secret you debate,
Like Turkish divan, or Venetian peers;
Hatching infernal plots against the State—
Nay! good my Lords! I pay you spare my ears!

I never said, whilst here in state you sit,
Like Satan's Council, you're ten times as big,
Swoln by the magic of your self-conceit,
As folks that walk about without a wig.

I never said that you were bound to do
Aught else, but what your Lordships freely chose;
That states have any right to question you,
Or thrust in your concerns a busy nose.

"Satan's Council": " 'But far within / And in their own dimensions like them-
selves / The great Seraphic Lords, and Cherubim / In close recess and secret conclave
sat.' Milton. See the passage at length. Par. Lost, B. I., l 777 etc." (Editor).

89

I never questioned your undoubted right
To give what titles, and to whom you please;
You shall be dukes and princes! by this light,
I'll lie as quiet as a mouse in cheese.

I ne'er asserted that you ruled the bank;
Or said it had an influence over you:
You all shall be Directors; first in rank;
And if you please, kings, lords, and commons, too.

Gad so! my gracious lords, I've found at last
That I've been guilty of an indecorum:
In thus addressing you, I've been too fast,
I should have first addressed his worship Quorum.

Great Sir! but troth, this measure will not hit
The solemn style which I to him must use;
So, if you please, I'll stop a tiny bit,
And hold a conference with Madam Muse.

June 12, 1793

Ode IV
To a Would-be Great Man

Jonathan defendeth the great Defender; —magnifieth and exalteth his works, and confesseth his own littleness of understanding.

"Certat tergeminis tollere honoribus." Hor.

Daddy Vice, Daddy Vice,
The drift of your fine publication:
As sure as a gun,
The thing was just done
To secure you—a pretty high station.

"To a Would-be Great Man": Vice-President John Adams.
"your fine publication": Adams's "Discourses on Davila," printed in *The Gazette of the United States* in 1791.

Defenses you call
To knock down our wall,
And batter the states to the ground, sir,
So thick were your shot,
And so hell-fire hot,
They've scarce a whole bone to be found, sir.

When you tell us of kings
And such pretty things,
Good mercy! how brilliant your page is!
So bright in each line,
I vow now you'll shine
Like a glowworm, to all future ages.

When you handle your balance,
So vast are your talents
Like Atlas your wonderful strength is,
You know ev'ry state
To a barleycorn's weight,
For your steelyeard the continent's length is.

On Davila's page
Your discourses so sage,
Democratical numbskulls bepuzzle
With arguments tough,
As white leather or buff,
The Republican bulldogs to muzzle

'Tis labor in vain
Your senses to strain
Our brains any longer to muddle;
Like Colossus, you stride
O'er our noddles so wide,
We look up like frogs in a puddle.

June 19, 1793

91

Ode V
To a Truly Great Man

"Justum et tenacem propositi virum." Hor.

George—on thy virtues often have I dwelt,
And still the theme is grateful to mine ear:
Thy gold let chemists ten times over melt,
From dross and base alloy they'll find it clear.

Yet thou'rt a man—although perhaps the first;
But man, at best, is but a being frail;
And since with error human nature's curst,
I marvel not that thou should'st sometimes fail.

That thou hast long, and nobly served the State,
The nation owns, and freely gives thee thanks:
But, sir! whatever speculators prate,
She gave thee not the power t'establish banks.

No doubt, thou thought'st it was a phoenix nest,
Which Congress were so busy to build up,
But there a crocodile had fixed his rest,
And snapped the nation's bowels at a sup.

The greedy monster is not yet half cloyed,
Nor will he, whilst a leg or arm remains;
These parts the last of all should be destroyed;
The delicious morsel is her brains.

I trust thou'st seen the monster by this time,
And hast prepared thy knife to cut his throat;
His scales are so damned hard, that in thy prime,
'Twould take thee twenty years to make it out.

"To a Truly Great Man": George Washington.

"morsel is her brains": "This prediction begins already to be in train to be fully accomplished. The American character for industry and sobriety begins to be lost in the rage of speculation" (Editor).

"twenty years": "The period for which the National Bank was established. The sums borrowed of it by the government are so many pledges of perpetuity to it" (Editor).

God grant thee life to do it! Fare thee well!
Another time examine well the nest,
Though of Arabia's spices it should smell,
It may produce some foul, infernal pest.

June 22, 1793

Ode VI
To Midas

Jonathan entreateth Midas not to starve the nation—proposeth a project for paying off the National Debt through the instrumentality of the S—y of the T—y.

Suae fortunae faber.

O greedy Midas! I've long since been told,
Whate'er you touched is instant turned to gold;
Thine alchemistic fingers, prithee, stop,
Or thou'lt not leave us all a single sop.

Those fingers from thy birth have been employed
With such well-timed precipitation,
That had the sacred college tried,
Thoud'st beat them all at transubstantiation.

Briareus had a hundred hands, but thou hast more,
Grasping at once this spacious globe around:
One hand embraces the Chinesian shore,
Beyond Ohio's banks another's found.

Mountains and rivers, rocks and sugar trees,
Nankeens and China, green and bohea teas,
Are instant turned to gold whene'er you please,
O spare untouched our codfish, rice and bacon,
Or else the continent must for forsaken.

"the sacred college": The Vatican.

93

Midas, much service might'st thou do the state,
Thy talents wert thou willing to exert;
Relieve the people from a grievous weight,
And give reward where there has been desert.

My project may appear a little bold;
But sure I am, 'twill pay off honest claims:
Touch H—n, and K—x, and F—r A—s,
And turn the speculators all to gold;
Let Congress send them straightway to the mint,
They'll pay our debts—or else the devil's in't.

June 29, 1793

Ode VII
To the Well-born

Under the type of the heathen gods Jonathan rehearseth the virtues of aristocracy.

Paree, precor, stimulis. Ovid.

Sons of Olympus, all! I kiss your hands,
A stately company, as I'm a sinner!
My little godlings! what are your commands?
I hope you do not mean to stay to dinner.

We've no ambrosia here—plain beef and mutton
Your Godships' stomachs will most surely turn;
Not for our whiskey would you give a button;
Such home-brewed nectar you will spurn.

We have no Ganymedes—no wanton Venus,
Nor ugly cuckold Vulcan, for a buff;
No pimping Mercury to go between us,
Or pick our pockets, or our purses cut.

"Touch H—n, K—x, and F—r, A—s": Alexander Hamilton, secretary of the treasury; Henry Knox, secretary of war; Fisher Ames, congressman from Massachusetts. All were accused by the Republicans of speculating in government script.

We have no Jupiter, with lust unbounded,
Our fair Alcmenes to seduce,
No drunken Bacchus with his tuns surrounded;
No Mars, God wot! can we produce.

We have no Proteus changing every hour,
As with his whim or interest stands,
No greedy Saturn to devour
His children in the midwife's hands.

We for your playmates have no little Cupid
To shoot at people when they're off their guard:
We mortals, truly, are so stupid
To think such treatment were a little hard.

Such fit companions you'll not find I swear;
Then why the devil should you tarry here?

Each embryo Romulus and Alexander,
So eager now to fill Fame's hundred trumpets,
Would deem it neither crime nor slander
To prove their virtuous mothers strumpets;
If bastards they will be reputed
Of gods that had their dads cornuted.

Ye would-be Phaetons, now so intent
To mount, and set us in a blaze,
    Or drive us to the devil and all;
Trust me, you'd better be content,
For, ere you've tried it many days,
    By G— you'll get a fall.

July 3, 1793

"We have no Proteus": "Jonathan is certainly mistaken—we have a number of them" (Editor).

Ode VIII
To Minos

—————*Jura Silentibus*
Reddit.—————. Ovid.

Stern judge of shades! revisit'st thou this earth
To try us all, ere we have crossed the Styx?
Not only punishing our childish tricks,
But damning us, by wholesale, from birth!

As mortal bodies, states, no doubt, have souls,
Which brings them all within thy jurisdiction;
And since no earthly judge thy voice controls,
They must be damned, without a legal fiction.

Thine eminent domain, what state opposes,
Or dares remember it was sovereign once!
Since to the grindstone thou hast brought their noses,
Thoul't leave among them not a single sconce.

Their little corporations all sh'all melt
In the hot crucible that holds thy brains,
Till not a single particle remains
Of all the fancied sovereignty they've felt:
    A voice shall then be heard in Congress Hall
    States are no more—and we are all in all!!!

July 20, 1793

"Minos": Chief Justice John Jay.

"our childish tricks": "The hasty measures adopted by some of the states at the commencement of the late Revolution, which cooler politicians have since condemned" (Editor).

"eminant domain": "It has been asserted by the most grave and learned authority of Judge Minos, that by the right of eminent domain, the United States, even before the adoption of the present Constitution, might by their treaties annul the acts of the states, although at that time unquestionable sovereign" (Editor).

Ode IX
To Liberty

Jonathan addresseth his castoff mistress—pretendeth to have forgotten her name—revileth her groveling taste, furious temper and contempt for her betters—commandeth her not to disturb the peace, and driveth her beyond the Atlantic: but at parting seemeth half willing to be reconciled to her again.

> *In vitium Libertas excidit*————*Hor.*
> *Et Tuba terribilem Sonnitu Tarrantantara*
> *dixit*————. Virg.

O Thou! whatever be thy doubtful name,
Once dear to us, and still to Gallia dear,
Whose boisterous accents, fill the trump of Fame,
Accents which we have grown too deaf to hear:

Who didst, erewhile, in Congress Hall preside,
Each vote dictating to prevent mistakes,
Though now thine image there be thrown aside,
Doomed to oblivion in a filthy jakes:

Who didst in many a well-fought battle wave
Thy bloodstained banners o'er our fainting heads,
And from the jaws of death and ruin save
Full many a wight, that now thy presence dreads:

Who, when the din of war no more was heard,
Didst to the humble cottage straight retire,
And to imperial palaces preferred
Bar independence round a rural fire:

"thy doubtful name": "That which in a democracy, is called Liberty, in governments of a different nature, obtains the epithets of licentiousness, anarchy, etc. Hence arises Jonathan's embarrassment by what name to call his *quondam* mistress" (Editor).

"thine image": "The removal of the bust of Liberty from the Federal Hall to the watercloset, where the members when hardpressed retire, is a fact well known in Philadelphia, though perhaps not generally known elsewhere. Trifles, says Dr. Franklin, are like straws—they sometimes serve to show which way the wind blows" (Editor).

Who, when thou'rt wooed, art as a virgin mild,
Thine angel-visage all bedecked with smiles;
But when opposed, like a hyena wild
Thy savage fangs! —whose rage no art beguiles;

Who dost like death on all conditions look,
Nor spar'st a Stuart's or a Capet's head;
Nor fear'st this earth must some convulsion brook
For them; as if Tom Thumb the Great were dead;

Who at one stroke, hast thousands beggars made,
Of those whose Fortune's minions were before,
And left them, without wealth, or worth, or trade,
To starve—as they had millions starved before:

Who carest no more for coronets, or crowns,
Or any modern would-be lordling cit,
Alike condemning both their smiles and frowns,
Than if our Daddy-Vice had never writ——

Avaunt! —Nor let thy clarion grate our ears
With sounds, terrific as the final trump!
Sounds which once turned our pruning hooks to spears,
And from their scabbards caused our swords to jump:

Sounds! that should Congress listen, might appall
The stoutest champion there for right divine;
Recall thine image back to Federal Hall,
And to thy temple turn corruption's shrine:

Sounds! that might even tempt them to reward
The care-worn soldier's fears and wounds and woes,
Though S—h and A—s should think the measure hard,
And speculators turn from friends to foes:

"those whose Fortune's": "The aristocrats of France" (Editor).

for right divine "The doctrine of *jure divino* right, though exploded for a century, seems likely to be revived in our days, if the views and wishes of certain friends to monarchy among us should prevail" (Editor).

"S—h and A—s": William Smith, congressman from South Carolina, and Fisher Ames, congressman from Massachusetts, both ardent Federalists and both accused of speculating in script.

Sounds! that perchance might e'en the Senate wake
From dreams of rank and titles, power and wealth;
Or bank director's gilded slumbers break,
And bring the Constitution back to health:

Sounds! that perchance might to the states recall
Some faint remembrance of lose sovereign rights,
Those rights, which mighty Atlas doomed to fall,
And which stern Minos banished from their sights:

Sounds! that might peradventure drive away
The faithful Britons from our western posts;
Those sentinels, who guard us night and day,
Our scalps defending from the Indian hosts:

Sounds! that perchance might prompt a silent wish
To aid their struggles, who once aided ours;
Nor, whilst thy cause is fighting, mute as fish
Behold the ambition of combining powers:

To France return!!! There shall thy brazen lungs
Yield music, sweeter than the Syren's voice,
Though louder far than Fame's twice fifty tongues,
And unborn millions at the sound rejoice.

"lost sovereign rights": "Several of the states proposed amendments on the subject of the judicial department of the government of the United States, which have been entirely disregarded hitherto by Congress. Since this Ode was first published Congress have, however reluctantly, recommended an amendment in this respect" (Editor).

"right, which mighty Atlas doomed": "See Ode II. Whether Atlas [Hamilton] penned the draught of the present Constitution or not, it is well known to have been his policy to annihilate the states, and in lieu of a Federal Republic, to erect an energetic monarchy" (Editor).

"Minos": Chief Justice John Jay.

"who once aided ours": France.

There, wave thy banners! —there thy falchion wield!
There, lead to victory each gallant son!
There, let thy slaughtered foes bestrew the field!
Nor let e'en tyrants, there, thy vengeance shun!

Nay—though imperial crowns, and heads should fall,
Nor age, nor sex protect thy fiend-like foes,
Rather than thou should'st quit this earthly ball,
E'en Jonathan shall cry—God speed thy blows!!!

Aug. 14, 1793

Ode X
To the Democratical Society of Philadelphia

Jonathan reproveth the impertinent views of that institution—
prophesieth concerning a would-be great man. —By comparison with
the heavenly bodies, showeth the respective merits of the great
heads.

Per insidias iter est, formasque ferarum. Ovid.

Sons of sedition! say, what do you here,
Where peace and loyalty unrivaled reign?
Where wealth rewards the speculator's care,
And rank and place your groveling arts disdain.

"fiend-like foes": "For shame Jonathan! would'st thou doom to the guillotine
such heads as the Empress of all the Russias?" (Editor).

"Democratical Society": "For the objects of this instutition, see the *National
Gazette*, No. 179" (Editor). The Democratic Society of Pennsylvania was one of many
such societies organized in 1793 on the model of the French Jacobin clubs. It reflected
the ardent sympaties of Americans for France and the French Revolution, and advo-
cated an alliance with France. It had Jefferson's support and Hamilton's opposition.
Because of its support of Genet, it incurred the wrath of Washington, who denounced
it in his message to Congress the following year (1794). Tucker, of course, favored
the Society. See last note to "A Supplementary Ode," page 105.

Go watch the sun! —see his unfading light
Since time begun still unobscured remain!
Go watch his beauteous sister-orb of night!
Go watch the planets which compose his train!

Go plant your telescopes against each star
Whose radiant sphere illumes the vast profound!
Some blemish amongst them, shall easier far,
Than in our bright galaxy here, be found.

Not less in luster, as not less in size,
Than a dim planet to the orb of day,
Lo! next that height, to which he ne'er shall rise,
Our Vice like Mercury pursues his way.

Scowling malignant on the Indian plains,
Intent to set their wigwams all on fire,
See K—x like ruddy Mars his course maintains
Through lions, scorpions, and chimeras dire.

Hugest of planets that adorns our sphere,
Refulgent in his triple, golden zone,
See H—n like Jupiter appear,
With satellites around his paper throne.

Whilst on those minor orbs his light he sheds,
That borrowed light on him shall they reflect:
Nor whilst he pours down blessings on their heads,
With incense to repay shall they neglect.

"watch the sun": "David Rittenhouse, Esq. if not the first, at least among the first astronomers which the world has produced since the immortal Newton, was President of the Society" (Editor).

"our bright galaxy": "See certain strictures on this institution in Mr. Fenno's Gazette" (Editor).

"K—x": Henry Knox, secretary of war.

"triple, golden zone": "Head of the Treasury; ruler of the Bank; commissioner of foreign loans" (Editor).

"H—n": Alexander Hamilton.

Removed beyond the reach of vulgar eyes,
As far as human brains or thoughts aspire,
The self-illumined Minos sweeps the skies,
Like Saturn, freezing, midst his ring of fire.

Yon concave vast behold! where wolves and bears
And geese and foxes all together meet;
Say, if less bright, our Congress Hall appears,
Prepared for George to take his annual seat?

Cease then, ye elves of darkness, cease to pry
Into those secrets you're forbid to know;
Content yourselves to scrutinize the sky;
Presume not to enquire what's done below!

Aug. 9, 1793

Aug. 21, 1793

Ode XI
To Atlas
Being the Second Part of Ode II

Jonathan recanteth his former errors: —discloseth the secrets of a great assembly: —again doubteth, and concludeth with an apt simile.

Atlas! 'Tis true that once I said
You prop the states up, with your head;
   But I was wrong to do't:
My recantation, then believe,
And trust me, what I now perceive,
   You've trod them underfoot.

"Minos": Chief Justice Jay.
"Saturn": "The orbit of Saturn being at an immense distance from the sun, it is generally supposed that the temperature of that planet is as cold as that of Mercury is hot. The temperature of Mars is supposed to be less ardent than his ruddy look would indicate" (Editor).
"wolves & bears": "The names of several constellations" (Editor).
"Prepared for George": "It is then only to be seen in its full lustre; some of the most brilliant constellations being invisible at all other periods" (Editor).
"Atlas": Alexander Hamilton.

102

'Twas you that in Convention first
Pronounced the government accurst,
    Whilst sovereign they remained:
Then boldly moved to knock them down,
And crush them all beneath a throne,
    Or, to it have them chained.

Sure, 'twas enough to strike them dumb,
To put them under sheriff's thumb,
    Like culprits vile and base:
What tho' they are not hang'd as yet;
Still, two to one, perhaps, you'd bet,
    That it will be the case.

But after all—no doubt, I rate
Too high your influence in the state,
    Nay, I'll be sworn, 'tis so:
The town clock tells us when we dine;
The weights that move its hands and thine
    Play out of sight, below!

Aug. 11, 1793

                          Aug. 28, 1793

"have them chained": "This fact has been so often asserted, without being ever contradicted, that there can remain little doubt of its authenticity" (Editor).

It will be the case": "Execution, says Lord Coke, is the end of the Law: it would have been happy for America, had the Convention reflected how this end was to be obtained against a state" (Editor).

Ode XII

Jonathan taketh his leave of his correspondents: apostrophiseth a great man without stain, and giveth to real merit, merit's due.

Majora canamus. Virg.

Enough of Atlas! and the venal train
That 'round his paper shrine attendant meet:
Enough of Daddy Vice's fertile brain,
Titles and rank Prolific to create,
    Prolific as Egyptian oven vast,
      Where chickens, ducks and geese are hatched so fast!

Enough of the well-born! those lordling cits,
Who now presume so high to hold their heads:
Wretches, whose pride by far outweighs their wits,
Who, if they know, try to forget their dads;
    Just as rank weeds that on a dung-hill grow,
    Shoot up at once to hide the filth below,

As the philosopher in search of truth
With high contempt each base deception spurns;
As from the midnight punk the generous youth
To the chaste object of his passion turns;
    As from a loathed disease returning health;
    Or, as from beggary the joys of wealth;

As to the blind the newfound bliss of sight;
As to the galley-slave fair freedom's hand;
As from a dungeon the return of light;
As from a shipwreck the long wished for strand; —
    My soul turns from them all with high disdain
To find in George true greatness without stain.

O Washington! for whom my willing lyre
    Unbidden vibrates loudest notes of praise
When shall thy yet unrivaled worth inspire
    Some emulations of thy glorious days!

"Atlas": Alexander Hamilton.
"Daddy Vice": Vice-President John Adams.

Still, as a father to thy country dear,
Regard not those who seek to wound thy peace,
Nor to their impious falsehoods lend an ear,
Who would persuade thee her regards can cease.
　　Still at the helm go on our bark to steer,
　　Nor quit it, till thou leave thine equal there.

Aug. 12, 1793

Aug. 31, 1793

A Supplementary Ode

Heu, quam difficile est crimen non prodere. Ovid.

Tussis pro crepitu, no doubt an art is,
Not easy to translate in decent phrase;
But understood and practiced by the parties
That would be uppermost in modern days.

Thus moderate men, who twenty years ago
At independence frowned and made wry faces,
Of mother Britain's rights made much ado,
Meant nothing more, than just to keep their places.

So when our soldiers perished on the decks
Of prison ships, —or died by exaltation,
Vile Tories, trembling for their forfeit necks,
Loudly exclaimed against retaliation.

"thine equal there": "Perhaps it would have been happier for his truly venerable character if he had rather listened to the advice of Horace in the following lines, '*Solve senescentem mature sanus equum, ne / Peccet extremum'*, / than to the advice of those who flattered themselves that he would descend to the grave with glory unobscured" (Editor).

"an art is": "For the original definition of this art, the reader is requested to refer to Hudibras, Canto 1, line 830, etc." (Editor).

"died by exaltation": "For the number of American prisoners privately executed in New York, see the confession of one Cunningham, a British deputy commissary, who not long since met with his proper reward in the same way" (Editor).

So when our Daddy Vice bewrought his brain
To tell us all of lords, and dukes, and kings,
No doubt His Worship counted all the gain
Which from preeminence and title springs.

So when our our triple-headed Publius barked,
Like Cerberus, at unbelieving Anty,
Each proselyte-monger for himself had marked
Of federal loaf and fish no portion scanty.

Thus A—s and S—h so eager to repair
The tattered remnant of our public credit,
To patch the garment better, thought it fair
On their own meager carcasses to spread it.

Thus Atlas to support his paper throne,
And give its faithful guards another sop,
To pay off France, proposed a further loan,
Gaps of instrumentality to stop.

Thus Antigallicans and British mongrels
Who at republican successes sweat,
Buzzing like swarms of flies from fifty dunghills,
Have neutrals turned to vilify Genet.

"Daddy Vice": "If there be any office under the federal government perfectly
superfluous, it is surely that of Vice-President, except in the event of the President's
death or removal from office. At all other times the office may strictly to be said to
confer *otium cum dignitate*. The Senate might certainly have been entrusted with the
choice of their own Speaker, from among their own body" (Editor).

"Publius": "There is an illiberality in some of the letters of Publius that dis-
graces the admirable talents displayed throughout that work" (Editor). Publius was the
name assumed by Hamilton, Jay, and Madison as authors of *The Federalist* (1788).

"A—s" and "S—h": Fisher Ames and William Smith. "The whole credit of this
beautiful piece of patch-work is not exclusively due to these gentlemen. *Locus est
pluribus umbris*" (Editor).

"British Mongrels": "Those who having professedly become citizens of the Un-
ited States, retain their former devotion to the British, and antipathy to republican gov-
ernments. Of these the poet says, '*Coelum, non animum, mutant*' " (Editor).

"Genet": "As Jonathan is neither acquainted with the full measure of the crimes
imputed to the French Ambassador, nor heard anything either in vindication or denial
of the charges against him by Mess. Wilcox and Co. he waits to be better informed
than he is at present, before he presumes to join the fraternity above described as buz-
zing about his nose" (Editor). Genet had incurred the wrath of Washington by attempt-
ing to arouse public support in Philadelphia for the cause of the French Republic.

106

As Witches, hating people, to torment 'em
Stick pins in images that represent 'em.

And now, good folks, a dozen odes I've writ
(More by one-half than e'er I thought to write)
And if I have not always shown my wit,
No doubt you'll say that I have shown my spite:

Foe to all party but the public weal,
All secondary motives I disdain;
For ne'er shall worth my smarting satire feel,
Nor vice a plaudit from my hand obtain.

Farewell! perhaps when next our Congress meets,
Amongst them I may take a little peep;
Not to disturb their worships in their seats,
But just to see who wakes, and who's asleep.

Sept. 7, 1793

John Jay was appointed minister to England in April, 1794, and departed on May 12 to negotiate a treaty with Prime Minister Grenville. The result was the unpopular "Jay's Treaty" which was made public in June, 1795. Tucker's poem, of course, was written before the treaty was drawn. The poem is from Ode XI, Part II, of The Probationary Odes.

A Trip to St. James's, 1794

Lend me thy trumpet Fame! thy brazen lungs,
Thine hundred mouths, and eke thine hundred tongues!
     My liver swells with vehement desire,
To tell such things as scarce will be believed;
Namely, the wonders that have been achieved,
          Without the aid of sword or fire,
But in a modest, decent, civil way,
By our Extraordinary Envoy, Mr. Jay.

Say, muse, 'midst what acclaims he did set out,
    Attended down to Whitehall stairs,
    By thousands in their Sunday airs;
Who when he got on shipboard gave a shout:
The mighty blast filled the *Ohio*'s sails,
Then homeward all the shouters turned their tails,
And left the ship in charge of Mr. Jay,
To sea-girt Britain's coast to make her way.

Swift as an arrow from an Indian's bow,
    The ship across the Atlantic shot,
Swifter than ever ship was known to go,
    And of her destination hit the very spot;
        As proud of such immortal honor
        As our great Envoy laid upon her;
Then to New York came straightway back to tell,
That in her charge she had succeeded well.

Now muse, let us return to Mr. Jay,
Who safe to London city found his way;
    With ceremonial due then went to greet
Grenville's new lord, and Billy Pitt likewise,
Who viewed the Envoy Ex with wondering eyes,
    Wondering what brought his Ex to Downing street;
Then promised soon to show him to the king,
To whom he might unfold the tidings he did bring.
Meantime Lord Grenville asks his Ex to dine,
An honor which his Ex could not decline:
There cheek by jowl with lords he sits in state,
With due decorum emptying every plate;
Then dinner done, the loyal glasses ring,
With loyal bumpers crowned, to George the king.
        Now mount, O muse, on eagle's wings,
        Attend with Mr. Jay the King of Kings.

The day was come, the weather wonderous fair,
When with Lord Grenville to St. James' Court
His Ex the Extra-Envoy did repair,
Of's errand and himself to make report.

The monarch saw—and turning to the queen,
"Look, look, there's Jay, there's Jay, there's Jay, I ween
From Congress come to make a bow;
I wonder if the dog knows how?"
His Ex advanced and made a bow by rule,
Which showed he had been at a dancing school;

The monarch then returned a monarch's nod,
Awful, no doubt, as the Olympian God;
When thus, in humble tone of supplication,
Did Mr. Jay begin his smooth oration.

"O Sire! permit a wight thy subject born,
His fellow subjects' sufferings to impart,
Nor from their wailings turn thine ear in scorn,
Like Egypt's king of old, of hardened heart.

"I did not like Moses come, with threats to fright,
Or daunt with spells and charms thy royal breast;
Our unfledged eagle, all too young for fight,
Sits, like the peaceful Halcyon, in its nest.

"She, like the peaceful Halcyon, went to glide
(If true the tale that's told of other times)
Borne on the azure bosom of the tide,
From shore to shore, from clime to distant climes.

"But mews and seagulls now disturb her rest,
And boobies strike her with their jobbernowls;
Voracious sharks assault her peaceful nest,
And warlike swordfish pierce it full of holes.

"Thou, who like Neptune, dost the trident sway,
Alone can'st quell those monsters of the main:
O! let thy clemency shine forth we pray,
And halcyon days prolong thy glorious reign!"

"mews and seagulls": The allusion in these and the following lines is to England's seizure of American ships under the "Orders in Council," and her impressment of seamen from American vessels.

109

Meanwhile, a gracious ear the monarch lent
To Mr. Jay, and eke his compliment,
To which he condescended such reply,
As Billy Pitt dictated, by the bye.
Next to the queen his Ex did make his leg,
And with the king her intercession beg;

To which the queen returned two royal dips,
Though not a word escaped her royal lips;
Then to each prince and princess low he bowed,
As demagogue, when he salutes the crowd.
This done, the monarch gave a gracious grin,
And thus familiar question did begin.

"Well! since your independence you have got,
Are you much happier than before, or not?
Good salaries, and sinecures! hae, Mr. Jay!
Or are republicans too stingy, pray?
Does Mr. Washington, hae, wear a crown?
No, no, not yet, not yet, you'd knock him down."

"Great sir," cries Mr. Jay, "We han't, as yet,
A head among us that a crown would fit."
"No, no, I guess not," instant cried the king,
"His head, I'm sure's not fit for such a thing;
You're all republicans, hae, Mr. Jay,
All *sans-culottes*, no doubt, aye, aye, aye!"

To which his Extra-Ex did make reply,
In tone so sweet the king could but believe:
"Permit me, sire, your ears to undeceive;
That all are *sans-culottes* I dare deny,

Nor need I further prove what I advance,
Since I am here, O king, and not in France."
The monarch, half-convinced, exclaimed "Egad!
If you were there, you'd chance to lose your head:
Han't you among you got the guillotine?
Yes, yes, I'm sure you have—myself and queen
Would soon among you all be lopt off short
As wheat in harvest—and as much in sport,

110

"I'm sure," cries Mr. Jay, in accents sweet,
Confounded by what majesty had said;
"Your sacred heads, more precious far than wheat,
From scythes, or guillotines have naught to dread."

"Godso! I doubt it much, upon my life!"
The sputtering monarch quick replied,
"A lowly tailor (can it be denied!)
Among you kicked my son that kissed his wife."
"That fact," cries Mr. Jay, "I can't deny."
"No, no, no, that you can't, I, I, I, I!"
The monarch said, "for Neddy swore 'twas true.
And that the tailor beat him black and blue."

The blushing queen here turned her head aside,
Blushing in part with shame, in part with pride;
Each bashful princess hung her lovely head,
And seemed to sympathize with brother Ned.

Now Billy Pitt and Grenville's lord began
To fear the monarch might betray the man;
For monarchs can sometimes like parrots talk,
As monkeys, on two legs, like monarchs walk.

So Grenville plucked the envoy by the sleeve,
And whispered it was time to take his leave.

Oct. 1794   1796

"beat him black and blue": "This kicking and crudgelling is said to have been
bestowed upon the young prince in Vermont" (Editor).

This is a jubilant election victory poem, written on March 3, 1801, the day Adams left office, and the eve of Jefferson's inauguration.

For the Washington Federalist
A New Federal Song

The Jacobins have got the day
    The Feds are homeward moving;
But when they come again this way,
    There will be desperate shoving.

Yankee doodle, keep it up,
Yankee doodle dandy,
The Feds will never start a peg
Till cider turns to brandy.

Duke Braintree is to Quincy gone,
    To study new defenses,
For spite of all the old he finds,
    The folks have lost their senses.

Yankee doodle, etc.

There's Sedgewick quits his lofty seat
    For better speculation,
Than can be found while surly Smith
    Will print the Fed's orations.

Yankee doodle, etc.

The election of 1800 had resulted in a tie between Jefferson and Burr, the Democratic-Republican candidates, who each received seventy-three votes. The Federalist candidates, John Adams and Charles Pinckney, had received sixty-five and sixty-four votes, respectively. The Federalist-dominated House of Representatives, which had to decide the victor, favored Burr, but Hamilton backed Jefferson, who received a majority vote on the thirty-sixth ballot. Burr became vice-president.

"Duke Braintree": John Adams. Braintree was the original name of Quincy, Adams's birthplace.

"Sedgewick": Theodore Sedgewick (1746-1813), speaker of the House of Representatives, 1788-1801.

"Smith":?

There's Dayton gone to see his lands
    And have them all surveyed, sirs,
But shortly he'll be here again,
    With sword and black cockade, sirs.

Yankee doodle, etc.

There's Wolcott, he gives up the cash,
    To sit upon the bench, sirs:
Like Felix, 'round the Jacobins
    He'll work till he is weary.

Yankee Doodle, etc.

There's Otis leaves seditious laws,
    To be the Fed attorney;
When in your tails he sticks his claws,
    You'll wish the de'il to burn ye.

Yankee doodle, etc.

There's Griswold, he won't condescend,
    To be war secretary;
But if you trust him with the cash
    He'll work till he is weary.

Yankee doodle, etc.

    "Dayton": Jonathan Dayton (1760-1824), Federalist leader from New Jersey. In 1799 and 1800 he was involved in land frauds.
    "Wolcott": Oliver Wolcott (1760-1833), Adams's secretary of the treasury.
    "Felix": "See Hogarth's humorous picture of St. Paul preaching before Felix. 'And when he reasoned of righteousness, and judgement to come, Felix trembled.' Acts of the Apostles" (Tucker).
    "Otis": Harrison Gray Otis (1765-1858), congressman from Massachusetts (1797-1801). He became district-attorney for Massachusetts in 1801.
    "Griswold": Roger Griswold (1762-1812), congressman from Connecticut (1795-1805). Just before Adams left office, he offered Griswold the post of secretary of war, but Griswold declined.

There's Dexter fit for any thing;
    Can preach on any text, sir;
Let John or Jefferson, be king,
    You'll find him Ambidexter.

Yankee doodle, etc.

There's Read, and Green, and Hill, and More
    Are all turned into judges,
For not a Fed, without a place,
    From Congress homeward trudges;

Yankee doodle, etc.

But Bayard, he won't go to France
    To see his gallant cousins,
Lest Heaper's wonderous tales and plots,
Should multiply by dozens,

Yankee doodle, etc.

There's Hamilton, he lies perdue,
    With old sly Pickering, sirs,
In spite of all the fools can do,
    They soon will have a kind, sirs.

"Dexter": Samuel Dexter (1761-1816), secretary of war from June to December, 1800. He started as a Federalist but shifted his support to Jefferson.

"Read, and Green": "Not room enough to name half" (Tucker). These were the so-called Midnight Judges, appointed by Adams just before he left office.

"Bayard": James Bayard (1767-1815). In another of his last official acts, Adams appointed Bayard minister to France, but Bayard declined.

"Harper": Robert Goodhoe Harper (1765-1825), Federalist senator (1795-1801). The allusion is to his pamphlet, *Observations on the Dispute Between the United States and France,* published in 1795.

"Pickering": Timothy Pickering (1745-1829), Adams's secretary of state.

Yankee doodle, etc.

Then, we shall sing, "God Save the King";
    Th' aristocrats and Tories,
And placemen all from south to north,
    Will join, in joyful chorus.

Yankee doodle, keep it up,
Yankee doodle dandy,
The Feds will never start a peg
Till cider turns to brandy.

Mar. 3, 1801

A New Song

Merino sheep! Merino sheep!
   Come, who will buy Merino sheep!
Merino sheep! now going cheap!
   Oh! what a chance to make a sweep!
And have a flock of Merino sheep!

Merino sheep! Merino sheep!
   A thousand dollars for a sheep!
Merino sheep! I needs must weep,
   To see them going all so cheap!
Oh! why did I bring Merino sheep!

Merino sheep! Merino sheep!
   Why sure, good folks, you're all asleep!
You will not buy Merino sheep!
   Though now they're going all dog cheap!

Merino sheep! Merino sheep!
   A thousand dollars for a sheep!
An hundred dollars for a sheep!
   Come make a sweep, they're quite dog cheap,
Come, fifty dollars for a sheep!

It makes me weep, they are so cheap,
   Come, twenty dollars for a sheep!

Come, take the whole and make a sweep
   At fifteen dollars for a sheep!
And you shall have Merino sheep.

Merino sheep! Merino sheep!
Come, who will buy Merino sheep!
What glorious profits shall he reap,
That now will buy Merino sheep!
       Merino sheep!

Merino sheep! Merino sheep!
Who wants a flock of Merino sheep!
Oh! What a chance to make a sweep;
And get a flock of Merino sheep!
    Merino sheep!

Merino sheep! Merino sheep!
A thousand dollars for a sheep!
Why sure, good folks, you're all asleep,
That you won't bid for Merino sheep!
    Merino sheep!

Merino sheep! Merino sheep!
Though here we offer them so cheap,
A thousand leagues across the deep,
We've brought these fine Merino sheep!
    Merino sheep!

Merino sheep! Merino sheep!
An hundred dollars for a sheep!
It makes me weep, they are so cheap!
Why won't you bid for Merino sheep!
    Merino sheep!

Merino sheep! Merino sheep!
Come, fifty dollars for a sheep!
Come make a sweep! They're quite dog cheap
And you shall have Merino sheep!
    Merino sheep!

Merino sheep! Merino sheep!
Come, thirty dollars for a sheep!
Come, take take the whole and make a sweep,
At twenty dollars for a sheep,
    Merino sheep!
Come take the whole and make a sweep
At twenty dollars for a sheep!
    Merino sheep!

[1810]

117

On Reading a Letter From a Very
Sprightly Lady, Disclaiming All Ideas of
Love, and Matrimony, to a Particular Friend

More tranquil than the western breeze,
Which fans in spring the blooming trees,
My breast (the lovely Delia cried),
Will ever be, on the left side,
    Where Cupid's arrows enter.
Agreed! the sprightly Laura said,
But, tell me, thou dear charming maid,
    How is it, ——at the center?

Apr., 1810

The Virginia Patriot's Invitation
to His Customers

Come all who love a savory dish,
    Here's codfish, cheese, and liver!
There's no such liver, cheese, or fish,
    South of Potomac river.

'Tis wholesome food for every day,
    And for a feast on Sunday,
It is superior every way,
    To New York salmagundi.

Whoever tastes this wholesome dish,
    Shall strait grow wondrous wise;
For, like the gall of Tobit's fish,
    It opens blindmen's eyes.

"Virginia Patriot": "This was the title assumed for Davis's Virginia Gazetter, by
one Livermore, a bitter Yankee printer from Boston, by whom that paper was con-
ducted for some time" (Tucker).
"Salmagundi": "The title of a periodical paper in great repute in New York"
(Tucker). The paper, whose name comes from a New England hash, was really a
series of pamphlets by Washington Irving, William Irving, and J. K. Paulding, all
Federalists. They were published in 1807.

Some Yankee cheese, as story tells,
    Killed all the Havana rats;
Our dish, that famous cheese excells,
    Destroying Democrats.

All ye who now refuse to store
    Yourselves with such a hoard,
Nor codfish, cheese, nor Livermore,
    Shall ever grace your board.

Apr., 1810

"Havana rats": "This fact was mentioned in many newspapers, and occasioned a general prohibition of American cheese from being imported into Havana" (Tucker).
    "Livermore": "Mr. Livermore was in great request among the Federalists in Richmond, dining with them frequently, which gave rise to this trifle" (Tucker).

PATRIOTIC POEMS

On General Washington

When Alcides, the son of Olympian Jove,
Was called from the earth, to the regions above,
The fetters grim Tyranny burst from his hand,
And with rapine, and murder, usurped the command:
While Peace, lovely maiden, was scared from the plains,
And Liberty, captive! sat wailing in chains;
Her once gallant offspring lay bleeding around,
Nor, on earth, could a champion to save her to be found.

The thunderer, moved with compassion, looked down,
On a world so accurst, from his crystalline throne;
Then opened the book, in whose mystical page,
Were enrolled the heroes of each future age:
Read of Brutus, and Sidney, who dared to be free;
Of their virtues approved, and confirmed the decree;
Then turned to the annals of that happy age,
When Washington's glories illumined the page.

"When Britannia shall strive with tyrannical hand,
To establish her empire in each distant land,
A chief shall arise, in Columbia's defense,
To whom the just gods shall their favors dispense:
Triumphant as Mars, in the glorious field,
While Minerva shall lend him her wisdom, and shield:
And Liberty, freed from the shackles, shall own,
Great Washington's claim, as her favorite son."

Aug. 26, 1780

1780

120

Benedict Arnold, commander of West Point, had conspired with Major John André, a British officer, to turn over to the British the plans of West Point, but the scheme failed when André was captured on September 25, 1780. Arnold fled to the British and André was executed as a spy on September 30.

On General Arnold

At Freedom's call, see Arnold take the field,
With Honor, blazoned on his patriot shield!
His gallant deeds a dazzling luster spread,
And circling glories beamed around his head.
But, when estranged from Freedom's glorious cause,
Renouncing Honor, and its sacred laws,
Impelled by motives of the basest kind,
Which mark the vicious, mean, degenerate mind;
To virtue lost, and callous to disgrace,
The traitor hiding, with the hero's face;
His cankered heart, to sordid views a slave,
To Mammon yielding all that freedom gave,
Enleagued with fiends of that detested tribe,
Whose god is gold, whose savior is a bribe,
Could basely join, his country to betray,
And thus restore a ruthless tyrant's sway;
On freedom's sons impose the galling yoke,
And crush each foe to vice, beneath the stroke;
Not all his laurels in the field obtained!
Not all that Philip's son, by conquest gained!
Not all that once adorned great Caesar's brow!
Nor, all that Washington may challenge now!
Could save a wretch, whom crimes, like these, debase,
So far beneath the rank of human race!

"On General Arnold": Tucker wrote on the manuscript, "These lines, I have lately discovered, have found a place in Franklin's Memoirs, vol. I, p. 406. See also p. 408, 409." The poem appears at the end of a letter to Franklin, dated Oct. 12, 1780. The author, whose name is not given, introduces Tucker's poem with these words: "The annexed, a specimen of American poetry, well describes the popular feeling on the occasion." Since the writer knew of Tucker's poem by Oct. 12, Tucker must be in error as to the date of composition.

But, stung with keen remorse, his guilty soul,
In vain, shall seek repose, from pole to pole;
Perpetual anguish shall torment his breast,
And hellish demons haunt his troubled rest;
Not even death shall shield his hated name,
For, still, the caitiff shall survive to fame;
By fate's decree! who thus pronounced his lot:
"Too bad, to live! too base, to be forgot!
Thy crimes succeeding ages shall proclaim,
And Judas be forgot, in Arnold's name!"

Oct. 25, 1780

In the summer of 1781, General Cornwallis led a raid into Virginia in an attempt to destroy the supply and training bases of the American forces. He almost captured Governor Thomas Jefferson and the legislature at Charlottesville.

The Progress of Cornwallis
An Irregular Ode

I

Bellona's thunder rends the western skies,
The din of battle shakes the troubled air;
    Sounds of frantic horror rise,
    Shrieks of woe, and wild despair;
Through Carolina's laurel groves,
Secure, the prowling Briton roves,
And mocks the foe, and fate defies;
    Since, prostrate on the ground,
    O'erwhelmed with many a wound,
In agonizing pangs Rebellion gasping lies.

"Rebellion gasping lies": "At the period alluded to, the British never spoke of the Americans but as rebels and the Revolution as a rebellion" (Tucker).

II

See Terror stalking through th' affrighted land!
Grim Rage, and fell Revenge his steps pursue,
Rapine, and harpy Famine join the band,
    The wretched victim's dying groans
    The widowed matron's tender moans,
    The virgin's plaints, the orphan's cries,
    Ascend, in concert, to the skies:
There hollow Want in secret anguish pines,
No more relieved from Plenty's cheering hoard;
Here pale disease the parting breath resigns,
And Desolation waves around her flaming sword!

III

    See the gorgon foe advance!
    See him couch his quivering lance!
    Thine, Virginia: next to feel
    The fatal vengeance of his steel:

    Thine, with terror to survey,
    His splendid host in dread array:
    Thine, beneath is power to languish,
    Torn with rage, despair, and anguish!

IV

In her car triumphant riding,
'Midst ten thousand glittering spears,
Through the liquid azure gliding,
Bright-eyed Liberty appears.

Far renowned in martial story
See a chief her faulchion wield!
Beaming with celestial glory,
Lo! a monarch bears her shield!

Britain! thy short triumphal course is run!
Thy flitting glories vanish from the sight;
Lost in the radiance of a brighter sun,
Like falling stars they're seen, 'midst darkness, only, bright.

June, 1782

Ode to Peace

Come, sweet Peace, and with thee bring
All the odors of the spring;
Summer's golden harvests, too,
Autumn's fruits of various hue,
Winter's health, and cheerful fires,
Joys, which competence inspires.

Leave to war the vernal blights,
Scorching summer's sultry nights,
Autumn's fogs, and sickly dew,
Rugged winter's blustering crew,
Slavery, famine, and despair,
Leave behind to cruel war.

All the good that freedom brings,
Mirth from innocence that springs,
Temperance, the foe to strife,
Friendship, sweetest balm of life,
Love, that rivals bliss divine,
Gentle Peace: be ever thine.

1787-1788   1790

On June 22, 1807, Captain Douglas of His Majesty's Navy, commanding the Leopard, stopped Captain Barron's Chesapeake and demanded permission to board and search the ship for British deserters. When Barron refused, Douglas opened fire, killing three and wounding eighteen American sailors. He then boarded the American ship and took off four alleged deserters. On July 2, the day Tucker composed the poem, President Jefferson issued a proclamation ordering British warships to leave U.S. waters. Tucker notes on the manuscript that "These lines were spoken by Mr. Wirt, at the Capitol in Richmond at the celebration of the Fourth of July . . . in 1807."

On Hearing of the Attack Made by
the British Captain Douglas, of the Navy,
on the Chesapeake, Commanded by Commodore Barron,
in June, 1807, Near Cape Henry

Tyrant! again, we hear thy hostile voice!
    Again, upon our coast thy cannons roar!
For peace, again, thou leavest us no choice!
    Again, we hurl defiance from our shore.

Hast thou forgot the day that Warren bled,
    While hecatombs around were sacrificed?
Hast thou forgot thy legions captive led?
    Thy navies blasted, by a foe despised?

Or, think'st thou we've forgot our brothers slain!
    Our aged fathers weltering in their gore!
Our widowed mothers, on their knee, in vain,
    Their violated daughters' fate deplore!

Our towns in ashes laid! Our fields on fire!
    Our wives and children flying from the foe!
Ourselves in battle ready to expire:
    Yet struggling still to strike one other blow!

Know then this day recalls the whole!
    Now, hear our solemn, and determined voice:
In vain proud tyrant! shall thy thunders roll;
    Since, once more, victory or death's our choice.

July 2, 1807

When the year 1809 began, England and France had been at war for a year, and would fight on for five more years. The United States, then only in her teens, was constantly embroiled in disputes with both France and England over the freedom of the seas. (See "On Hearing of the Attack . . . on the Chesapeake.")

Ode
For the new year—1809

Still, Bellona's thunders roll,
Rend the earth, and shake the pole!
Europe smokes from east to west;
    Gaul and Britain feed the fires;
Tyranny erects its crest;
    Freedom from her shores retires.

Hail Columbia! happy land!
    Peace, with liberty be thine!
But, would Freedom's voice command,
    Instant, at the call divine,
    Rush to glory, at her shrine!

Freedom! endless by thy sway!
Boundless, as the solar ray!
Peace the consort of thy reign;
Virtue foremost in thy train;
Wisdom thine unerring guide;
War and tyranny defied.

Hail Columbia! happy land!
    Peace with liberty be thine!
But if Freedom's voice commands,
    To arms! To arms! To arms!
Instant, at the call divine,
    To arms! To arms! To arms!

Rush to glory at her shrine!
    Rush to glory!
    Rush to glory,
        Rush to Glory, at her shrine!

(If such the will divine),
    Fall, with glory!
    Fall, with glory!
    Fall, with glory, at her shrine!

Jan 1, 1809

This poem was probably inspired by the reactions of both France and England ("insulting foes") to the U.S. Embargo Acts of 1808, and the Enforcement Act of 1809. Designed as economic weapons against those nations, the acts were openly flouted by both France and England.

Union March

Rise, Columbia rise! For peace hath lost its charms!
    Hark from afar,
    The clang of war!
    Insulting foes
    Your rights oppose:
Rise, Columbia rise! 'Tis freedom calls to arms!

Rise, Columbia rise! Let union arm your bands.
    From east to west,
    Her high behest,
    Let all obey:
    In dread array
Rise, Columbia rise! 'Tis freedom's voice commands.

Rise Columbia, rise! At freedom's sacred shrine,
    Your vows renew:
    Swear to be true
    To Liberty!
    And still be free!
Rise, Columbia rise! Be death or freedom thine.

Feb. 26, 1809

Lines Written Soon After the Declaration of War Against Great Britain, in June, 1812, When Congress Passed an Act for Raising Troops.

To the Friends and Supporters of Liberty, and Their Country.

Remember the days, when fair Liberty's call
    Roused the sons of Columbia to arms;
When we swore, one and all, at her altars to fall,
    Ere a tyrant should rifle her charms:
When Montgomery, Warren, and Mercer the brave,
    Sealed the thrice-solemn oath, with their blood;
And Washington, destined his country to save,
    Swept off all her foes, like a flood,

Remember, when Freedom her banners unfurled,
    And exalted her standard on high;
We swore to defend her against the whole world,
    And for her, to conquer, or die:
Bunker's Hill, Saratoga, Kings Mountain, and York,
    Attested the truth that we swore;
Independence, and union, and peace, crowned our work;
    And Liberty triumphed once more.

Now, when insolent tyrants assail her again,
    And traitors are plotting her fall,
Shall the bliss-giving Goddess invoke us, in vain,
    Like lions to rouse at her call?
Remember our oath! And remember the blood,
    That sealed the dread oath, that we swore!
And remember the days, when victorious we stood!
    And conquer for Freedom, once more.

Aug. 7, 1810

The first draft of this poem is dated August 15, 1810. Perhaps the poem was then inspired by the actions of the British navy against American shipping. But when the poem was published, in 1814, the United States had been at war with England for two years. In September, the month before the poem was published, British forces had burned Washington (August 24-25) and attacked Baltimore. Their unsuccessful seige of Fort McHenry this same month was the inspiration for Francis Scott Key's "The Star Spangled Banner."

Invocation
Addressed to Every Friend of His
Country; September 1814

Sons of freedom! who have bled,
Where Washington or Warren led,
Over heaps of mighty dead,
    'Gainst a tyrant enemy;
See again: The battle lower!
Britain rallies all her power—
Now descends a fiery shower!
    Cannons roar, and rockets fly.

Shades of patriots in the grave!
Shades of parted heroes brave!
Born, your country's rights to save,
    From a ruthless tyrant's sway!
Rouse your gallant sons to arms!
Bid them wake to freedom's charms!
Bid them rush to war's alarms!
    Rouse! And drive their foes away.

Bid them hasten to the strand!
Sword to Sword, and hand to hand!
    Suffer not a foe to land
    On the shores of Liberty!
Back to ocean drive the slaves!
There to perish in its waves!
Sink them to their watery graves!
    Worthy not on earth to die!

129

Sons of patriots in the grave!
Sons of parted heroes brave!
Born, your country's rights to save
    From a ruthless tyrant's sway;
Be not blind to freedom's charms!
Be not deaf to war's alarms!
Rouse ye! rouse ye! quick to arms!
    Rouse ye! and drive your foes away!

Haste ye! haste ye! to the strand!
Sword to Sword, and hand to hand!
Suffer not a foe to land
    On the shores of liberty!
Back to ocean drive the slaves!
There to perish in its waves!
Sink them to their watery graves!
    Worthy not on earth to die!

Aug. 15, 1810   Oct. 5, 1814

TALES

Humps and Robin
A True Story

Oh muse, who didst ere while inspire
The merry strains of Matthew Prior,
Descend and to my pen indite
A tale, which Matt, alone, should write
    Travelers and poets long ago
Have claimed the privilege, you know,
Of changing persons, time and place,
To give their tales a better grace,
Or to conceal from observation
The real truth of their narration:

130

Resolved this method to pursue,
We mean to deal in fiction too,
As far as names and places go,
The rest our tale shall truly show.

Near to a place whence royal George,
Of this rebellious land the scourge,
One of his oldest titles gains,
There lived a youth the pride of swains,
Whose swelling calf and back of brawn,
Might cause a dowager to pawn,
Her richest jewels for a sample
Of strength and nerve beyond example:
Yet sooth to say, our simple Humps,
Although he held a hand of trumps,
Knew not the value of his cards,
Nor thought them worth his least regards,
Until a lass of comeliest mold,
Who twice nine years had scarcely told,
His dormant faculties excited,
Whence, she in turn was well requited.

Humps like another Timon felt,
His heart for Iphigenia melt,
To Robin, first of wags, he goes
His strange condition to disclose,
The symptoms felt by youthful lovers:
Rob tells him, wedlock is the pool
In which his raging flames must cool;
Humps grinned assent. The lass, tho' coy,
At length consents to wed the boy.

Suppose the wedding day arrived
And honest Humphrey fairly wived,
The dinner ate, the dancing ended,
The bride by all her maids attended,
Slip out unseen, and half undressed;
Robin who dearly loved a jest,
Once more takes honest Humps aside
T'instruct him how to greet the bride.
Quoth he— "What's to be done tonight,
"Friend Humphrey, is a solemn rite,
"At Hymen's altar 'tis expected
"That not one state should be neglected,

131

"Then let an offering go round
"For each, with due libations crowned."
    A message broke the conversation
And Humps retired to his station:
Like Milton, we too highly deem
Of nuptial beds to follow him.
Then here we choose to draw the curtain,
Nor dare to speak of things uncertain.
    With folded arms and settled gloom
Next morning Humps came in the room,
While Robin smoked his second pipe:
The wag, for mischief ever ripe,
Asks how the posset-bowl held out?
Humps sheepish looked—then turned about,
And said, "Though not a drop was wasted,
"Nine times, alone, the cup I tasted:
"Four states, alas! unblessed remained,
"The posset-bowl was fairly drained."
Quoth Robin— "Your libations's short,
"Indeed I fear, by half a quart;
"Tonight the matter may be mended,
"Take t'other bowl when one is ended."
Humps thanked him for his good advice
And swore he'd drain the goblet twice,
    Next morn, again with clouded brow,
Humps meets with Robin at the plough.
"Alas," he cries, "my worthy friend
"Where will my disappointments end?
"Though twice the posset-bowl was crowned,
"Nine times, alone, the toast went round;
"The vain attempt I must give o'er,
"I fear I ne'er can reach the score."
Quoth Robin— "Though there's much to fear,
'Tis best to hope and persevere."
    Thus Humps each morn did Robin shrive,
Until the score got down to five;
Then Humps, with looks more sad than ever,
"My friend, I've done my best endeavor
"My feeble force again to rally
"I can not rise beyond a tally,

"My dear, my lovely Iphigene
"Must surely sink into the spleen,
"Thus of expected bliss beguiled,
"She'll think she's wedded to a child:
"Nor here concludes my sad disaster
"I need a poultice, or a plaster,
"What was no larger than my wrist
"Is scarcely smaller than my fist."
     "Adzooks," quoth Robin—"never mind,
"A hair of the same dog you'll find,
"A better poultice to apply,
"Than any plaster you can buy."
     Humps groaned assent—but doubted much
Whether the poultice he could touch.
     Two days had passed since Robin heared,
How now with honest Humps it fared,
At noon he finds him still in bed,
With rueful face, and drooping head,
To every kind enquiry dumb,
He neither finger raised nor thumb.
When Robin thus—"Why what a pother
"You make of things which any other
"Would think but very moderate duty.
"Your Iphigene, too, such a beauty!
"You should at least the score have doubled,
"Nor at a trifle thus be troubled.
"There's a neighbor Charles—ten years age gone
"Since duty was to him but fun;
"Eight bumpers are his common dose,
"Less will not lull him to repose,
"And if perchance he lacks his score,
"Next night he takes a bumper more."
     Humps groaning raised his eyes and said,
"Ah! Robin—would that I were dead!"
Just then a tittering laugh betrayed
His Iphigene behind the bed.

Nov. 8, 1788

The Tobacco Pipe

The wag to mischief who's inclined
To that, alone, gives up his mind,
And sacrifices foes or friends,
Without regret, to gain his ends.
　　Where Roanoke rolls its limpid tide
Through fertile fields on either side,
Not long ago there was a wedding,
Where guests were plentier far than bedding.
A stranger, I forget his name,
Who from a distant county came,
At all events must have a bed;
For Robin, Harry, George, and Ned,
A pallet on the floor was spread,
The clock struck twelve—to rest they went,
And till the morning slept content;
But Robin with the lark arose
In haste, and to the garden goes:
Then uprose Harry, George, and Ned,
The stranger, fast asleep, in bed,
Lay all uncovered on his face,
Not dreaming of his foul disgrace;
His hapless case when Harry found
He casts his wicked eyes around.
Takes Robin's pipe from off the shelf
(The stem a reed, the bowl was delft),
And to the stranger's nether eye
The taper point he doth apply,
And shoves it in, up to the bowl,
So well he understood the hole:
Dan Prior's ladle not more quick
In old Corisca's bum did stick;
Then out again the reed he takes,
Before the abused stranger wakes:
But had not time the stem to wipe
When Robin came to seek his pipe,
And presently begun to smoke,
Quoth Harry— "Don't you smell a joke?"
Robin threw down the pipe in haste,

And spitting cried, "Some smell, some taste:
"They're both so strong—so may I thrive,
"They'll last as long as I'm alive."

Nov. 27, 1788

The Faithful Mastiff
A True Story

At lukewarm, or at faithless friends
        I've no design to rail:
An honest, but mistaken zeal,
        The subject of my tale.

Yet think not, with a cynic's eye
        That I regard mankind
Because in men and brutes, alike,
        Some qualities I find.

To err is human—and that dogs
        Can be mistaken too,
Most clearly follows from a tale
        Which I can vouch is true.

Ah! could I but as clearly prove
        That men, like dogs, were true,
Full many a heart would now be blithe,
        Which now their falsehood rue.

In Williamsburg, 'ere party rage
        The capital removed,
Together lived three waggish sparks
        Who mirth, and frolic loved.

Their names are still remembered there;
        For, still, some there remain,
To curse that policy that razed
        Their city to the plain.

Their house by night from thieves to guard
    A mastiff they had bred;
Yet, oft, did honest Towser go
    The way their footsteps led.

For well he knew their waggish tricks
    Might sometimes kindle rage,
And well he knew the argument
    That passion to assuage.

For he had found a single look
    From him could peace command,
As readily as did the touch
    Of Hermes' magic wand:

Or, as the intercessions strong
    Of well-armed faithful friends,
Or, as the sheriff's puissant arm,
    When *posse com.* attends.

One evening in the month of June,
    When sultry was the day
To Waller's Grove our youngest wag
    Directs his lonely way:

That Grove, where old Dodona's pride
    Spread far and wide its shade
Till war and avarice allied
    A cruel havoc made.

His steps the faithful Towser marked
    As on he saw him pass,
And followed lest perchance there lurked
    Some snake beneath the grass.

When night her sable mantle spread
    The youth a cottage spied,
Where to solace from earth-born care,
    With nimble pace he hied.

There, lived a nymph whose tender breast
    Was ne'er assailed in vain;
Delighting pleasure to impart
    To all who felt a pain.

Our weary pilgrim in the bed
    Now sought a soft repose;
When Towser straight crept underneath,
    And fell into a doze.

The creaking bedstead roused him soon;
    A rustling noise he hears
Of conflict fierce above his head,
    And for his master fears.

He bounces up—and seized the foe,
    Beyond the bended knee,
Nor, heeds, that in the conflict, low,
    And panting, laid was she.

"Why how now, Towser!" cried the wag.
    "Pray let us both alone:
"Your aid, just now, I do not want,
    "My adversary's down."

Dec. 24, 1789

The Author's Muse to the Reader
A Monitory Tale

In fair Barbados once there dwelt a dame
Of special note, though I forget her name;
With flatulencies she was oft oppressed,
They soured her temper and disturbed her rest.
At length a grand specific she had found,
'Twas lemonade, with aqua-vitae crowned.
A nutmeg o'er the potion should you grate
'Twould make it punch; and punch the dame did hate.
One morning when the clock had just struck nine
She calls to Betty with a sickly whine.
"This dreadful colic—something I must take."
"A little spirit, madam, shall I add?"
"Yes to be sure! Why sure the girl is mad!
"Can pungent acids with my colic suit
"Unless there's spirit to correct the fruit?"
"A little nutmeg, madam—will you try?"
"Punch in the morning! Gracious God, I die!
"Think you with nasty punch I would get drunk!
"Begone you vile, abominable punk!"
         Now listen reader! punch if thou dost hate
         Shut up the book before it be too late
'Twas wholesome lemonade I meant to brew,
But troth I fear there's nutmeg in it too.
So, gentle reader, if thou dost get tipsy
Pray call me not a saucy wanton gipsy.

Jan. 1, 1790

The Cynic

Whoever to finding fault inclines
Still misconceives the best designs:
Praxiteles in vain might try
To form a statue for his eye;
Appelles too would pain in vain,
And Titian's colors give him pain,

138

Palladio's best designs displease him,
And Handel's water piece would freeze him,
Not Tully's eloquence can charm,
Nor e'en old Homer's fire warm:
On all occasions still a beast
He frowns upon the genial feast,
Swears that Falernian wine was sour,
And rails at champagne for an hour,
Not Heliogabalus's cook
Could drop a dish at which he'd look.
    Anticipating time and fate
He views all things when past their date,
Destruction in his noodle brewing
Turns palaces to instant ruin:
Speak but of Paris or of London
He tells how Babylon was undone:
Ask him, with Thais if he'll sup
He cries— "The worms will eat her up."
    Once at a merry wedding feast
A cynic chanced to be a guest;
Rich was the father of the bride
And hospitality his pride.
The guests were numerous and the board
With dainties plentifully stored.
There mutton, beef, and vermicelli
Here venison stewed with currant jelly,
Here turkeys robbed of bones and lungs
Are crammed with oysters and with tongues.
There pickled lobsters, prawn, and salmon
And there a stuffed Virginia gammon.
Here custards, tarts, and apple pies
There syllabubs and jellies rise,
Ice creams, and ripe and candied fruits
With comfits and eryngo roots.
Now entered every hungry guest
And all prepared to taste the feast.
Our cynic cries— "How damned absurd
To take such pains to make a —!"
Jan. 1, 1790

The Ass Turned Witness
A Tale—from La Fontaine

A painter jealous above measure,
The better to secure his treasure,
Above the keyhole of the place
That held it, paints a little ass.
    The sequel how shall I reveal?
A brother painter came to steal;
The door unlocks—but in his haste
The ass was totally effaced,
Except the head; which would betray
That somebody had been that way:
In haste his pencil then he got,
And drew another on the spot.
    Now see our jealous painter come
To view his exhibition room.
"Ye Gods, what here! Upon my life
I'm robbed!" he bawls out to his wife.
"No mortal has been near the place,"
Quoth she. —"My witness is the ass."
"The ass! you jade! My brains you'll addle:
Zounds! gypsy, who put on the saddle?"

Feb. 14, 1790

The Impossibility,
or, Old Nick Outwitted
A Tale—from La Fontaine

A devil once, as stories tell,
The most malicious fiend in hell
In solemn form of compact made
A bargain with an amorous blade:
The spark was by his aid to gain
A nymph for whom he sighed in vain;
Old Nick no recompense would have
But to remain his humble slave,
The youth was only to command
Whenever Satan was at hand,

140

Nor must his orders be delayed
When smutty face his visit paid,
His sole condition was dispatch
For Satan's ever on the watch;
Herein, whene'er the lover faltered
The case should instantly be altered:
Old Nick might drag him to his hole
And roast his body with his soul.

    Our lover laughed at the condition;
"Command is easier than submission:
"Obedience were another thing:
"What evil from command can spring!"

    Old Nick was faithful to his word
The lover shortly was preferred,
And 'midst his amorous caresses
His sooty benefactor blesses.

    Think of him and his horns appear:
Old Nick was straightway at his ear;
The lover sends him on an errand,
'Twas presently performed I warrant;
Whether to Italy or Spain
Satan was quickly back again.
Returned—our lover bids him go
And bring some gold from Mexico;
Then sends him off across the line
For jewels from Golconda's mine:
Behold, at once, a monstrous hoard
Of gold and jewels on the board!
Next sends to Canada for furs,
Satan was not in need of spurs:
A centaur's hide—a dragon's claw,
A mermaid's skin—a griffin's paw,
A craken's tooth—a phoenix' nest,
In turn, were instantly possessed.
"What! here again! Nay, this is Malice;
Go—build a temple or a palace."
Not Pandemonium more quick
Was raised without the aid of brick.

Our frighted lover now bethought him
That Satan in his trap had caught him;
For not a moment did he lose,
Nor leave the lover time to choose.
What service next to send him on
Before the last command was done.
The promised feast he scarce had tasted
And half the night in vain was wasted,
Nor could he hope by night or day
To keep the smutty fiend away,
And while he thought upon his talons
He lost all appetite for dalliance,
Thus with perpetual care oppressed
He to the nymph the whole confessed.
        "And is this all!" she smiling said,
"That has our mutual Bliss delayed!
Here—bid him straighten this"—she cried,
"And lay your silly fears aside."
Then put into his hand a hair
Which she had plucked the Lord knows where;
Whether from cushion, or from wig,
Or from stuffed hoop so round and big,
Or from her eyebrow, or from her temple,
'Tis certain it was but a sample;
As by the sequel will appear.
Old Nick was in a moment there;
For now he thought, that half an hour,
Would give his prey into his power.
"Here straighten this"—the lover cried,
Old Nick t'his mouth the hair applied:
The hair curled not a whit the less.
Ha! this won't do! We'll try a press.
A press, a vice, a weight in turn
He tries in vain—he's yet to learn;
He souses it into the ocean,
He might as well have drunk a potion.
In his own element he tries it,
Then on an anvil stoutly plies it;
Nor fire, nor water, press nor weight
Could make the curling tendril straight:

'Tis vain to tamper with it longer
It only makes the buckle stronger.
    No wonder if our spark was pleased
To find himself at length released,
For Satan came no more that night
But stayed until the morning light.
"Here, take your hair!" The tempter cries,
"It both my toil and skill defies;
Our bargain now is at an end."
The lover laughed and said—"Old friend
You're in a hurry to give o'er
I've just now found ten thousand more."

Feb. 18, 1790

The Discontented Student
A True Story

Returned from college R— gets a wife
To be the joy and comfort of his life:
But ere the honeymoon was in the wane
He sighs for college and his books, again
To his thought on all occasions flock:
Like Madam Shandy, thinking of the clock.
But, sad mishap! when Phoebus gilds the skies,
If to his favorite authors he applies,
Bright Venus throws her cestus o'er the book;
In vain he tries upon the page to look;
As Cupid blind, the classic page no more
Delights his raptured sight as heretofore.
Like that sagacious beast, who placed between
Two cocks of hay—one dry, the other green,
Can neither taste; our scholar every night
Thinks of his books; and of his bride by light.
Untasted joys breed always discontents;
Thus to his sire, his rage the scholar vents.
"Would that in Italy I had been born,
And, early, of each vile encumbrance shorn,
Which now seduces all my thoughts away
From Classic studies or by night, or day.
Uninterrupted then I might have read
Or in my elbow chair, or in my bed;
Till drowsy grown, and nodding o'er the book
Upon the enchanting page I craved to look
And then in rapturous dreams renewed the joy
Till taking, I resumed the blest employ.
But now in vain I quit the genial bed,
My wife—a plague!—keeps running in my head
In ev'ry page I read my raging fires
Portray her yielding to my fierce desires."
    "G— d— your books!" the testy father said
    "I'd not give ——— for all you've read."

The Judge With the Sore Rump

"Serva tibi minas!"
   To a judge who was seated on high;
As (for some fatal crime)
He devoted some time
   To prepare the poor culprit to die.

"What's that about mine a—e?"
(Says the judge to Aquinas,
   And turned up his rump as he spoke)
"I've a boil on my bum,
Thrice as large as my thumb:
   And see here! —the boil has just broke!"

Says Aquinas— "I find
That your tortures behind,
   Are more than you threaten, by far:
So here end your farce,
And take care of your a—e;
   And let me get out of the bar."

Jan. 27, 1819

"The Judge With the Sore Rump": This poem begins a letter to John Coalter (Tucker's son-in-law and, like him, also a judge), dated Jan. 27, 1819. The manuscript (unsigned, but in Tucker's hand) is in the Grinnan Collection, University of Virginia.
   "Serva Tibi Minas": "Keep your threats for yourself" (Tucker).

INDEX OF TITLES